A Treasury of Thanksgiving

A Treasury of Thanksgiving

ILLUSTRATED POETRY, PROSE, AND PRAISE

Leland Ryken

PUBLISHING
P.O. BOX 817 • PHILLIPSBURG • NEW JERSEY 08865-0817

The entry for the hymn "Blest Be the Tie That Binds" is adapted from the entry published in Leland Ryken, *40 Favorite Hymns of the Christian Faith: A Closer Look at Their Spiritual and Poetic Meaning* (Phillipsburg, NJ: P&R Publishing, 2022), 39–42.

The entry for the hymn "Come, Ye Thankful People, Come" is adapted from the entry published in Leland Ryken, *40 Favorite Hymns for the Christian Year: A Closer Look at Their Spiritual and Poetic Meaning* (Phillipsburg, NJ: P&R Publishing, 2020), 108–11.

Cover art is taken from Pieter Bruegel the Elder (ca. 1525–1569), *The Harvesters*, 1565, oil on wood. Courtesy of the Metropolitan Museum of Art, New York. www.met museum.org.

Printed in the United States of America

Library of Congress Cataloging-in-Publication Data

Names: Ryken, Leland, author.
Title: A treasury of thanksgiving : illustrated poetry, prose, and praise / Leland Ryken.
Description: Phillipsburg, New Jersey : P&R Publishing, [2023] | Includes bibliographical references and index. | Summary: "Thanksgiving is a yearlong Christian practice. In this lavishly illustrated anthology, Ryken presents forty great thanksgiving texts-Scripture, hymns, and prose-with helpful commentary and devotional remarks"-- Provided by publisher.
Identifiers: LCCN 2023016526 | ISBN 9781629959702 (paperback) | ISBN 9781629959719 (epub)
Subjects: LCSH: Thanksgiving Day--Religious aspects--Christianity.
Classification: LCC GT4975 .R867 2023 | DDC 242/.37--dc23/eng/20230824
LC record available at https://lccn.loc.gov/2023016526

For my grandchildren, with
gratitude:

Joshua, Kirsten, Jacob, Bethany,
Jack, Kathryn, Seth, Alison,
Meredith, Karoline, Annabelle,
Bradford, Pearla, Abigail,
Christianne, Mattaniah

Contents

previous: James Jacques Joseph Tissot, *Hide and Seek*, ca. 1877;
Camille Pissarro, *The Harvest, Pontoise*, 1881

Introduction

THIS BOOK OFFERS THE PROVERBIAL "two for the price of one." It is partly a seasonal collection that invites reading and contemplation as part of an annual Thanksgiving celebration. At this level, the entries can reacquaint us with familiar texts associated with one of the United States' favorite holidays. This is balanced by an educational aim to uncover little-known aspects of the history of the American Thanksgiving and its Puritan roots in Reformation England.

But this book is only partly seasonal. Gratitude and thanksgiving are not once-a-year activities. They are Christian virtues that God expects us to practice as a way of life. Accordingly, this anthology is a book for every day of the year—it is not a seasonal book only but a perpetual one.

Giving thanks does not come entirely naturally to us. It is something that we learn. That is why children need to be prompted with the question "What do you say?" when they receive a favor or compliment. The readings in this book are designed to foster our gratitude and thanksgiving in all situations.

Toward an Understanding of Thankfulness

The key to understanding the subject of this anthology is to picture a ladder. The bottom step of the ladder is our receipt of a favor or benefit that we cherish as a contribution to our well-being.

The next step is our recognition or awareness of this benefit. At this point the etymology of the word *thank* proves to be revealing. If we trace the word to its origin, we find that the root idea of thanks is *think*. A thoughtless person is not a thankful person. Before we can express gratitude for something, it needs to register in our thinking as something we appreciate.

At this point we face a choice, though we may not be aware of it. We can remain at the self-focused level, claiming possession of the benefit and going our self-centered way, or we can ponder the fact that we were sent the benefit from a source. It is not only something we receive but something we have been given. Ultimately, it always comes from God—usually also through some intermediary such as a person or a force of nature or a convergence of events.

Having (1) received a benefit, (2) experienced it as a positive infusion into our lives, and (3) acknowledged its source, we can ascend to the next

Paul Cézanne, *Still Life with a Ginger Jar and Eggplants*, 1893–94

step on the ladder, which is gratitude. Gratitude is something that we feel within ourselves. It is likely to be awakened only when we acknowledge the source of a blessing, but it stops short of expressing thanks to that source. Feeling grateful is a prerequisite to giving thanks.

Thanksgiving—the giving of thanks—takes gratitude a step further. Our awareness of having received a benefit and our gratitude for it now flow outward to the source of the benefit. Thanksgiving is relational, as we express gratitude to a giver in word or action.

All of the entries in this anthology fall into the paradigm of the ladder outlined above. Some, as we will see, awaken our gratitude for a given blessing but stop there. In these instances, *we* are the ones who must nudge these texts into the realm of thanksgiving. For example, the hymn "Amazing Grace" is a statement of testimony that continuously awakens our gratitude for God's grace, but it does not explicitly give voice to that gratitude. The canon of thanksgiving hymns and poetry would be incomplete without this type of latent thanksgiving text.

Differentiating Thanks from Praise

For purposes of this anthology, it is important for us to keep the line of demarcation clear between thanks and praise. In principle, it is easy to distinguish a thanksgiving poem from a praise poem. A *poem of thanksgiving* is marked by (1) a description of blessings received and (2) a response of thanksgiving specifically for those blessings. A *praise poem* does not primarily record gratitude but instead extols the worthiness of God. Although praise poems may resemble poems of thanksgiving because they catalog benefits to a person or people, they have a different goal and orientation: their purpose is to contemplate the praiseworthy acts of God rather than to explore how these acts have benefitted a recipient.

Even though we can thus distinguish between poems of thanks and poems of praise, confusion arises because the vocabulary of praise is often used in hymns and poems that are actually expressions of thanks. In this anthology, I have done two things to ensure that unrecognized classics of thanksgiving are not overlooked. One is to use my explications to clarify how poems and hymns that are not traditionally included in the canon of thanksgiving texts nonetheless deserve to be. The other is to adapt public domain texts to make them fit a specific purpose and occasion—a common practice among editors and compilers of hymnbooks—in this case by occasionally changing the vocabulary of praise to that of thanks.

For any of my readers who might find this unsettling, a quick visit to the website *Hymnary* will reveal that most familiar hymns exist in numerous variants. My substitution of the word *thank* for *praise* in the hymn "We Praise Thee, O God, for the Son of Thy Love," for instance, is in keeping with common practice. In fact, many readers of this anthology will be familiar with a version of that hymn whose opening stanza develops the theme "we praise thee, O God, for the days of our youth," which is not only a modification of the original hymn but an addition to it.

The Nature of This Anthology

My primary goal as I compiled this anthology was to collect the forty greatest thanksgiving texts of the English-speaking world. The most obvious trait of the resulting collection is its variety. There is variety of genres, first of all. I did not set out to include specific genres but simply allowed them to assert themselves. As I did, the following genres emerged:

- psalm
- additional biblical passages, both prose and poetry
- hymn
- poem
- prayer
- novel
- sermon
- classic prose devotional text
- public proclamation and historical document
- diary entry
- creed
- catechism
- theology book

The principle of variety extends to the organization of this anthology as well. After I had determined the contents of the book, I divided the material into four sections of ten entries and placed an equal number of various genres into each. This arrangement ensures a pleasing variety and guards against monotony.

Each text is accompanied by a short analysis, or what literary scholars call an *explication*. One way to integrate the texts and explications is first to read a text, then to assimilate the accompanying explication as casting a retrospective look on the first reading of the entry, and then to reread the text through the lens provided by the explication. ■

John Whetten Ehninger,
October, 1867

Now Thank We All Our God

MARTIN RINKART (1586–1649)

Now thank we all our God
With heart and hands and voices,
Who wondrous things hath done,
In whom his world rejoices;
Who from our mothers' arms,
Hath blessed us on our way
With countless gifts of love,
And still is ours today.

O may this bounteous God
Through all our life be near us,
With ever-joyful hearts
And blessed peace to cheer us;
And keep us in his grace,
And guide us when perplexed,
And free us from all ills
In this world and the next.

All praise and thanks to God
The Father now be given,
The Son, and him who reigns
With them in highest heaven—
The one eternal God,
Whom earth and heav'n adore;
For thus it was, is now,
And shall be evermore. ▪

The Sargent Family, 1800

IT IS APPROPRIATE TO BEGIN this thanksgiving anthology with the exuberant hymn that is sung at the beginning of many Thanksgiving church services. The poem gives us just the right words to express what is inside us when we are primed to thank God for his blessings to us. On such occasions, we want to thank God now, not later.

The most infectious aspect of this hymnic poem is its "all out" exuberance. In the opening lines, for example, we do not simply *thank* God but do so with *heart and hands and voices*. This triad foreshadows a technique used throughout the poem of enumerating two, three, or more items as though one is totally inadequate to express a gratitude that is ready to explode. In the middle stanza, for example, having mentioned the hope that God will be *near us*, the poem goes on to pour out five more anticipated blessings—from *ever-joyful hearts* to freedom from *all ills*—in a stream of clauses.

After we have been caught up in this general spirit of thanks, it is natural for us to shift our attention to the content and organization of the poem. Its opening stanza is a summons to thank God, accompanied by expansive and open-ended blessings, such as *wondrous things* and *countless gifts* that date from our infancy in *our mothers' arms* to today.

The middle stanza shifts from corporate thanks to a petitionary prayer. In keeping with the hymn's theme of gratitude for blessings, this prayer is addressed to a *bounteous God*. A list of petitions may seem surprising in a hymn of thanks, but even as we ask that God will shower us with particular blessings, we are made aware that these blessings are already ours. Thus we experience the list as one of received blessings for which we are grateful.

The final stanza returns to an expression of thanks to God. All the stops of the proverbial organ continue to be pulled out, as (1) all three persons of the Trinity are named, (2) both earth and heaven are said to adore God, and (3) the time span of the stanza covers what *was, is now, and shall be evermore*.

One more surprise remains. This over-the-top hymn of thanks was forged in the crucible of utmost suffering. Its author was a Lutheran pastor in Ellenberg, Saxony, during the Thirty Years' War (1618–1648). He arrived the year before the war broke out and died the year after it ended. The walled city of Ellenberg was not only overrun three times by hostile armies but also subjected to famine and epidemic illness. During his pastorate in the besieged city, Martin Rinkart presided over more than four thousand burials, including that of his wife.

We can claim the devotional potential of this hymn by going with its flow and allowing its words to unleash our feelings of gratitude to God. ◼

Multiple websites note that this hymnic poem is a cornucopia of biblical references—as many as sixty or seventy in number. An evocative parallel to the poem as a whole is David's prayer when the people of Israel assembled to bring contributions for the building of the temple. After extolling God's greatness, David prayed, "Now we thank you, our God, and praise your glorious name" (1 Chron. 29:13). This hymn likewise begins, *Now thank we all our God.*

Jean-François Millet, *The Potato Harvest*, 1855

Bless the Lord, O My Soul

PSALM 103

Bless the Lord, O my soul,
   and all that is within me,
   bless his holy name!
Bless the Lord, O my soul,
   and forget not all his benefits,

who forgives all your iniquity,
   who heals all your diseases,
who redeems your life from the pit,
   who crowns you with steadfast love and mercy,
who satisfies you with good
   so that your youth is renewed like the eagle's.

The Lord works righteousness
   and justice for all who are oppressed.
He made known his ways to Moses,
   his acts to the people of Israel.

The Lord is merciful and gracious,
   slow to anger and abounding in steadfast love.
He will not always chide,
   nor will he keep his anger forever.
He does not deal with us according to our sins,
   nor repay us according to our iniquities.
For as high as the heavens are above the earth,
   so great is his steadfast love toward those who fear him;

as far as the east is from the west,
    so far does he remove our transgressions from us.
As a father shows compassion to his children,
    so the Lord shows compassion to those who fear him.

For he knows our frame;
    he remembers that we are dust.
As for man, his days are like grass;
    he flourishes like a flower of the field;
for the wind passes over it, and it is gone,
    and its place knows it no more.
But the steadfast love of the Lord is from everlasting to
        everlasting on those who fear him,
    and his righteousness to children's children,
to those who keep his covenant
    and remember to do his commandments.

The Lord has established his throne in the heavens,
    and his kingdom rules over all.
Bless the Lord, O you his angels,
    you mighty ones who do his word,
    obeying the voice of his word!
Bless the Lord, all his hosts,
    his ministers, who do his will!
Bless the Lord, all his works,
    in all places of his dominion.
Bless the Lord, O my soul! ▪

THIS IS A POEM OF SELF-ADDRESS, as highlighted by the speaker's command to his own soul in the opening and closing lines. It is also a poem of summons in which the speaker awakens *all that is within* him to take stock of God's blessings and respond to them with gratitude. The key to experiencing this psalm as a thanksgiving poem is to embrace its command, in line 5, to *forget not all his benefits.* If we heed this admonition, we avoid a great deterrent to gratitude, namely, taking blessings for granted.

The backbone of a psalm of thanks is the technique of the *catalog* or list. We will appreciate catalog-of-blessings psalms most accurately if in our thinking we transmute such verbs as *bless* and *praise* to the verb *thank.* In Psalm 103, the poet thanks God for his benefits, both personally and in the believing community.

Psalm 103 is so exalted in tone and expansive in scope that the clarity of its design might surprise us. The poem unfolds, stanza by stanza, according to the following outline: a threefold call to bless God; a catalog of five benefits from God in the speaker's and our own personal lives; God's acts of benefit in the life of Israel and by extension the believing community throughout history; the magnitude of God's forgiveness; the permanence of God's steadfast love in contrast to the brevity of human life; God's universal kingship. The magnitude of all this is breathtaking, but, in a master stroke, the poem ends in quietude: *Bless [or thank] the Lord, O my soul.*

As a psalm of gratitude, Psalm 103 has proved versatile in the life of the church. In some families it is a "birthday psalm" that is read during birthday celebrations. In some churches it is read at the conclusion of Communion services. In liturgical churches, it is an all-purpose poem for feast days.

The psalm's devotional takeaway is expressed in line 5, as it commands us not to forget but to remember God's blessings, to rehearse them to ourselves, and to be grateful to the great God who confers them. ■

The importance of not forgetting to thank God for the blessings he confers is declared in striking fashion in Romans 1, in which one of the indictments of sinful humanity is that those who rejected God "did not . . . give thanks to him" (v. 21).

Vincent van Gogh, *Wheat Field with Cypresses,* 1889

Our Bounden Duty to Give Thanks

BOOK OF COMMON PRAYER

It is very meet, right, and our bounden duty,
that we should at all times and in all places
give thanks unto thee, O Lord,
Holy Father, almighty, everlasting God.

Almighty God, Father of all mercies,
we your unworthy servants give you hearty thanks
for all your goodness and lovingkindness to us
and to all whom you have made.
We bless you for our creation and preservation,
and for all the blessings of this life.
But above all we thank you for your inestimable love
in the redemption of the world by our Lord Jesus Christ,
for the means of grace, and for the hope of glory.

Accept, O Lord, our thanks and praise
    for all that you have done for us.
We thank you for the splendor of the whole creation,
    for the beauty of this world,
    for the wonder of life,
    and for the mystery of love.
We thank you for the blessing of family and friends,
    and for the loving care that surrounds us.
We thank you for setting us at tasks that demand our best efforts,
    and for leading us to accomplishments that satisfy us.
We thank you also for those disappointments and failures
    that lead us to acknowledge our dependence on you alone.

Let us give thanks to God our Father
for all his gifts so freely bestowed upon us—
for the beauty and wonder of his creation,
in earth and sky and sea,
for our daily food and drink,
our homes and families and friends,
for minds to think and hearts to love,
for leisure to rest and play,
for health and strength to work,
for the communion of saints, in all times and places,
and above all for the great mercies and promises
given to us in Christ Jesus our Lord.

Almighty God, who sent your Son Jesus Christ
    to reconcile the world to yourself,
we thank and bless you for those
    whom you have sent in the power of the Spirit
    to preach the Gospel to all nations.
We thank you that in all parts of the earth
    a community of believers has been gathered together
    by their prayers and labors,
and that in every place
    your servants call upon your Name.

Above all, we thank you for your Son Jesus Christ,
for the truth of his Word and the example of his life,
for his steadfast obedience by which he overcame temptation,
for his dying through which he overcame death,
and for his rising to life again,
in which we are raised to the life of your kingdom. ▪

This collection of thanksgiving prayers puts into practice what Ephesians 5:20 commands: "[Give] thanks always and for everything to God the Father in the name of our Lord Jesus Christ."

Tᴀᴇ sᴛʏʟᴇ ᴏғ ᴛʜᴇ Bᴏᴏᴋ ᴏғ Cᴏᴍᴍᴏɴ Pʀᴀʏᴇʀ is the very touchstone of greatness. It combines clarity and elegance to produce in its prayers what the King James Bible calls the "beauty of holiness" (Ps. 96:9).

The majority of its prayers are petitionary, but prayers of thanksgiving are also interspersed throughout. These fall into two categories, one of which is represented by the selection for this reading. Dating all the way back to 1549, the Book of Common Prayer has always contained a category called "General Thanksgivings." These are prayers tied not to specific events but rather to the general flow of life. They can be prayed any day of the year and at any church service. They are perpetually up to date.

The prayer of the first stanza, with its quaint terminology of *bounden duty* (a duty that we are *bound* or obligated to perform), may well be the most famous statement about thanksgiving in the English-speaking world. One reason it is so famous is that it is part of the Anglican weekly (or daily) communion service. Those four lines can serve as an epigraph or motto for this entire anthology, which is based on the premise that it is *meet*, or fitting, that we should *at all times and in all places* give thanks to God.

Following this invitation to fulfill the duty of thankfulness, the entry's medley of prayers consists of an ever-expanding list of blessings for which we are grateful. As the list unfolds, the concept of thanks ceases to be a mere abstraction and instead becomes concrete and experiential. The successive items function as prompts to picture our own personal experiences of the things that are named. It is not *work* or *family* in the abstract for which we are grateful but *our* work and *our* family.

The most obvious virtue of this litany of thanks is its comprehensiveness. In fact, we would find it hard to name blessings that are not encompassed somewhere in the list. Particularly noteworthy is the balance it strikes between spiritual blessings and physical ones and correspondingly between the supernatural realm and the earthly one. We can correctly think of this composite passage as a complete guide to thankfulness.

It is hard to imagine a more useful thanksgiving devotional reading than this one. It first reminds us in memorable language that we should always give thanks to God. Then, because we find it hard to think of all the things for which we are thankful, the combined prayers come to our aid and give us the words with which to express our total thanks. ▪

The New Testament and Book of
Common Prayer, ca. 1636

Thankfulness in Action

SNAPSHOTS FROM FIVE OLD TESTAMENT STORIES

Noah

THEN GOD SAID to Noah, "Go out from the ark, you and your wife, and your sons and your sons' wives with you. . . . So Noah went out, and his sons and his wife and his sons' wives with him. Every beast, every creeping thing, and every bird, everything that moves on the earth, went out by families from the ark. Then Noah built an altar to the Lord and took some of every clean animal and some of every clean bird and offered burnt offerings on the altar.

Jacob

THEN JACOB AWOKE from his sleep and said, "Surely the Lord is in this place, and I did not know it." . . . So early in the morning Jacob took the stone that he had put under his head and set it up for a pillar and poured oil on the top of it. . . . Then Jacob made a vow, saying, "If God will be with me and will keep me in this way that I go, and will give me bread to eat and clothing to wear, so that I come again to my father's house in peace, then the Lord shall be my God, and this stone, which I have set up for a pillar, shall be God's house. And of all that you give me I will give a full tenth to you."

Hannah

AND IN DUE time Hannah conceived and bore a son, and she called his name Samuel, for she said, "I have asked for him from the Lord." . . . And they brought the child to Eli. And she said, ". . . For this child I prayed, and the Lord has granted me my petition that I made to him. Therefore I have lent him to the Lord. As long as he lives, he is lent to the Lord." . . . And Hannah prayed and said, "My heart exults in the Lord."

David

THEREFORE DAVID BLESSED the Lord in the presence of all the assembly [of those who had contributed to the building fund for the temple]. And David said: "Blessed are you, O Lord, the God of Israel our father, forever and ever. Yours, O Lord, is the greatness and the power and the glory and the victory and the majesty, for all that is in the heavens and in the earth is yours. Yours is the kingdom, O Lord, and you are exalted as head above all. . . . And now we thank you, our God, and praise your glorious name."

Daniel

THEN THE MYSTERY was revealed to Daniel in a vision of the night. Then Daniel blessed the God of heaven. Daniel answered and said:

"Blessed be the name of God forever and ever,
    to whom belong wisdom and might. . . .
To you, O God of my fathers,
    I give thanks and praise,
for you have given me wisdom and might,
    and have now made known to me what we
        asked of you,
    for you have made known to us the king's
        matter." ∎

NEARLY EVERYTHING THE BIBLE SAYS about thanksgiving consists of either exhortations to be grateful or lyric expressions of gratitude. But the Bible is not lacking in narrative accounts of people who were grateful, and their gestures of thanksgiving can serve as a model and an incentive to us.

Before we look at what unifies this reading's five passages, we should relish the variety of situations that they encompass. Noah gave thanks when he set foot on dry ground after having been afloat in the ark for over a year. Jacob's moment of gratitude came when he awoke the morning after God had established him as the recipient of the covenant bless-

ing during a nighttime vision. Hannah lent her son Samuel to the Lord after he answered her prayer by ending her barrenness. In contrast to this solitary woman's gratitude, David's thanks was given in his public role, as a king, for the generosity his nation had shown by contributing to the construction costs of the temple. After God saved Daniel from a tight spot by revealing to him the content and interpretation of a dream, Daniel became an inspired poet who celebrated his deliverance from death.

Rembrandt van Rijn, *Jacob's Ladder*, 1655;
Lorenzo Monaco, *Noah*, ca. 1408–10

We can find a preliminary point of unity in this variety. It is that life presents many, many occasions that can and should awaken our gratitude. Blessings that call for gratitude are not on a short prescribed list but reach to all of life. A second point of unity is that the inner bent of these biblical figures was to turn immediately in gratitude to God. They did not require a sermon on thankfulness to prompt them to give thanks. A harvest of thanksgiving grows from the seedbed of a grateful heart.

This mosaic of five passages confirms the accuracy of the ladder of gratitude that was offered as a paradigm in this anthology's introduction. Each of the individual dramas of gratitude began with a blessing that was sent from God and received by human beings. We can see from their ensuing actions that each of our heroes recognized both the magnitude of the gift and its divine giver. But the characters did not stop with this act of perception. They spontaneously moved from acknowledgment to thanksgiving. For each of them, turning upward to God was the obvious way to consummate the gratitude they felt.

When we accept that these stories offer their central figures as models for us, there are abundant ways for us to apply these passages. The five examples held before us are positive models for us to emulate in at least four ways: by taking note of the blessings that come into our lives, by acknowledging that God is the giver of all good and perfect gifts, by feeling grateful for life's blessings, and by promptly thanking God in word or action. ▪

The Bible offers further dramatic examples of people who responded with appropriate thanks when God acted mightily on their behalf. When Jonah found himself in the belly of the great fish, he composed a poem whose summary statement is "I with the voice of thanksgiving will sacrifice to you" (Jonah 2:9). All the Old Testament examples in this reading sound out this same voice of thanksgiving.

Peter Paul Rubens, *King David Playing the Harp*, ca. 1627–28;
Pendant with Daniel in the Lion's Den (Byzantine), 1200 or later

Thanksgiving

ELLA WHEELER WILCOX (1850–1919)

We walk on starry fields of white
And do not see the daisies;
For blessings common in our sight
We rarely offer praises.
We sigh for some supreme delight
To crown our lives with splendor,
And quite ignore our daily store
Of pleasures sweet and tender.

Our cares are bold and push their way
Upon our thought and feeling.
They hang about us all the day,
Our time from pleasure stealing.
So unobtrusive many a joy
We pass by and forget it,
But worry strives to own our lives
And conquers if we let it.

There's not a day in all the year
But holds some hidden pleasure,
And looking back, joys oft appear
To brim the past's wide measure.
But blessings are like friends, I hold,
Who love and labor near us.
We ought to raise our notes of praise
While living hearts can hear us.

1865

Full many a blessing wears the guise
Of worry or of trouble.
Farseeing is the soul and wise
Who knows the mask is double.
But he who has the faith and strength
To thank his God for sorrow
Has found a joy without alloy
To gladden every morrow.

We ought to make the moments notes
Of happy, glad Thanksgiving;
The hours and days a silent phrase
Of music we are living.
And so the theme should swell and grow
As weeks and months pass o'er us,
And rise sublime at this good time,
A grand Thanksgiving chorus. ■

WE CAN GET A HEAD START on mastering this poem if we take a preliminary view of its two bookends. Its first four lines preview what the entire remainder of the poem will elaborate, namely, our tendency to be grateful only for spectacular blessings while not recognizing small ones. Its last two lines make it clear that, although the poem encourages us to live lives of gratitude every day of the year, it is also what is called an *occasional poem* and has been written with the Thanksgiving season specifically in view. The poem thus invites us to expand our Thanksgiving celebration by including gratitude for commonplace things.

This reading sums up two common tendencies in thanksgiving poems. The first is simplicity. Most thanksgiving poems in this anthology spring

previous: Edgar Degas, *A Woman Seated beside a Vase of Flowers*, 1865 from the folk imagination and represent poetry for the common person. Ella Wilcox's "Thanksgiving" speaks directly to our hearts. The poem is easy to assimilate because it is constructed on a sequence of two-line units, with the first line of each having eight syllables and the second one seven. The result is an easily managed rhythm of thought.

But the poem is equally representative of thanksgiving poems in that it has an element of complexity below its simple surface. Often in this genre complexity consists of a counter theme to the main theme—a contrary thought that challenges conventional thinking. Usually this counter theme has the effect of a criticism or rebuke. The title of this poem seems to promise a "feel-good" thanksgiving theme, which is surely present, but a more prominent theme is one of rebuke for our inadequate, ungrateful attitude toward *many a blessing*.

The format by which the poem pursues this critique is that of problem and solution. Stanza 1 poses the problem: our common human tendency to strive for huge blessings while ignoring the small ones that flood our lives. With the problem posed, the next two stanzas subject it to more detailed analysis. There is a division of duties between these two stanzas. The first explores how daily cares and worry hide blessings from our awareness. The second, the middle stanza of the poem, claims that we acknowledge small blessings only in retrospect, thereby missing the opportunity to give joy to others when the blessings occur. The fourth stanza offers a solution to the problem: thanking God for everything. The final stanza offers an action plan based on what has preceded it, which is to resolve to make all of life *a grand Thanksgiving chorus*.

Bumper-sticker mentality offers us the cliché "Be thankful for small things." This poem subjects that thought to analysis at a more profound level, its impact enhanced by its verbal beauty.

To appropriate the wisdom of this poem, all we need to do is heed its admonition. ■

Ella Wilcox's poem exhorts us to give thanks for small and routine blessings as well as big ones. First Thessalonians 5:18 similarly commands us to "give thanks in all circumstances; for this is the will of God in Christ Jesus for you."

Marietta Minnigerode Andrews, *Daisies and Queen Ann's Lace*, 1890

New Light on Thanksgiving

JOHN DONNE (1572–1631)

Meditation on Psalm 6

WE SHALL FIRST CONSIDER David's thankfulness, that is, his manner of declaring God's mercy and his security in that mercy. . . . But why is it so long before David leads us to that consideration? Why has he deferred so primary a duty to so late a place, to so low a room, to the end of the psalm? The psalm has a penitential part, a petitionary part, and a sacrifice of thanksgiving. . . . The third part of the psalm, the giving of thanks, is deferred, or rather reserved, to the end of the psalm. . . .

Not that the duty of thanksgiving is less than that of prayer, for if we compare them, it is rather greater, because it contributes more to God's glory to acknowledge by thanks that God has given, than to acknowledge by prayer that God can give. But therefore might David be later and shorter here in expressing the duty of thanks, because being reserved to the end and close of the psalm, it leaves the best impression in the memory.

It is easy to observe that in the whole Book of Psalms, the force of a whole psalm is for the most part left to the shutting up; the whole frame of the poem is a beating out of a piece of gold, but the last clause is as the impression of the stamp, and that is what makes it a coin. And then also, because out of David's abundant manner of expressing his thankfulness to God in every other place thereof, the whole Book of Psalms is called a book of praise and thanksgiving, he might reserve his thanks here to the last place. . . . Because David would dismiss us with that which concerns him most, he chooses to end in thanksgiving. . . .

The love of God is not a contract or bargain; God looks for nothing by way of payment. And yet he looks for thanks. . . . To utter thanks to God is all that our performance of thankfulness [entails]. . . . God looks for nothing to be done in the way of exact payment, but yet, as a clockmaker bestows all his labor upon the several wheels that thereby the bell might give a sound, and that thereby the hand might give knowledge to others how the time passes, so this is the principal part of that thankfulness that God requires from us, that we make open declarations of his mercies, to the winning and confirming of others.

Prayer of Gratitude

O eternal and most gracious God, . . . even casual things come from you, and what we call fortune here on earth is known as providence above in heaven. Nature reaches out her hand and gives us corn, and wine, and oil, and milk; but you fill her hand before, and you open her hand that she may rain down her showers upon us. Industry reaches out her hand to us and gives us fruits of our labor for ourselves and our posterity; but your hand guides that hand when it sows and when it waters, and the increase is from you. Friends reach out their hands and prefer us; but your hand supports that hand that supports us. ■

THESE TWO PASSAGES FROM A famous Renaissance preacher and poet come from different sources and embody two tendencies of mind for which John Donne is noted: the analytic and the devotional.

The first passage is excerpted from a sermon on Psalm 6. In typical Donne fashion, he poses a problem and then engages his listener or reader in the mental process of reaching a solution. The problem that Donne poses is why David the poet waits until the end of a psalm to express thanksgiving. In posing this problem, Donne presents a major contribution to our finding thanksgiving in the Psalms.

Scholars have noted that lament psalms (the most numerous type of psalm) typically conclude with a statement of confidence in God and a vow to praise him. These divisions have the merit of precision, but when Donne combines them under the heading of thanksgiving, he makes an equally helpful point. By this seemingly simple maneuver, Donne opens the door for us to see a much larger element of thanksgiving in the book of Psalms than we usually do—including the category of lament psalms, where it is unexpected.

Once we have absorbed this contribution to our experience of the psalms, we can follow Donne's meditation on the importance of thanksgiving in the eyes of God. He supports his claim even by the psalmist's placement of the section of thanksgiving at the end of his psalm. Additionally, Donne leads us to see an element of public testimony in our own statements of thanks to God.

The prayer of gratitude at the end of the selection comes from a famous devotional book that Donne composed while on a sickbed so dire that his friends feared he would die. Here, too, Donne shows his bent toward originality. It is customary for us to thank God for blessings, but Donne pushes our meditation behind the blessings themselves to the processes by which God's providence produces them. In this view, we should be thankful for the providential process that lies behind a blessing as well as for the blessing itself.

These excerpts from Donne stand ready to give us fresh insights that can become our permanent possession. His commentary on the thanksgiving sections that conclude numerous psalms can revolutionize our experience of thanksgiving in the Psalms. Similarly, his prayer of gratitude can serve as a prompt for us to be thankful not just for gifts of providence but also for the process that lies behind those gifts. ▪

Psalm 104 serves as an immediate illustration of what has just been stated. It is a nature poem that celebrates the means by which God provides for his creatures. Following the contours of what Donne puts before us, we can read the poem as a psalm of thanksgiving, beginning with the poet's declaration, "Bless [or thank] the LORD, O my soul" (v. 1).

Pierre-Édouard Frère, *Interior with Woman Teaching Child to Pray*, ca. 1819-86

When All Your Mercies, O My God

JOSEPH ADDISON (1672–1719)

THERE IS NOT a more pleasing exercise of the mind than gratitude. It is accompanied with such an inward satisfaction that the duty is sufficiently rewarded by the performance. It is not like the practice of many other virtues, difficult and painful, but attended with so much pleasure that were there no positive command that enjoined it, nor any recompence laid up for it hereafter, a generous mind would indulge in it for the natural gratification that accompanies it.

If gratitude is due from person to person, how much more from a person to the Maker? The Supreme Being does not only confer upon us those bounties that proceed more immediately from his hand, but even those benefits that are conveyed to us by others. Every blessing we enjoy, by what means soever it may be derived upon us, is the gift of him who is the great Author of Good, and Father of Mercies.

If gratitude, when exerted towards one another, naturally produces a very pleasing sensation in the mind of a grateful person, it exalts the soul into rapture when it is employed on this great Object of Gratitude, on this Beneficent Being, who has given us everything we already possess, and from whom we expect everything we yet hope for.

When all your mercies, O my God,
My rising soul surveys,
Transported with the view, I'm lost
In wonder, thanks, and praise.

How shall my words with equal warmth
The gratitude declare
That glows within my thankful heart?
But you can read it there.

Your bounteous hand with worldly bliss
Has made my cup run o'er,
And as a kind and faithful friend
You doubled all my store.

Ten thousand, thousand precious gifts
My daily thanks employ;
Nor is the least a grateful heart
That tastes those gifts with joy.

When nature fails, and day and night
Divide your works no more,
My ever grateful heart, O Lord,
Your mercy shall adore. ■

LIVING DURING THE EIGHTEENTH-century neoclassic era, Joseph Addison was what was known in that age as a professional man of letters and was the cofounder of a famous literary magazine, *The Spectator*. For the August 9, 1712, edition of the magazine, Addison composed a two-part article consisting of a brief essay and an accompanying thirteen-stanza poem on the subject of gratitude. The poem became a familiar hymn that has appeared in nearly a thousand hymnbooks.

Numerous entries in this anthology are built around the premise that giving thanks is a duty that God expects and commands. An unintended effect of this chorus may be to cause giving thanks to seem like a chore. The stark contrast Addison presents to that attitude may well startle us. He proposes that giving thanks is such a pleasurable experience that we can scarcely restrain ourselves from doing it. Accordingly, we can assimilate his essay as a corrective to a common misconception.

The accompanying poem that Addison composed puts his essay into practice. The vocabulary and sentiments possess an "all out" exuberance. Some examples include the claims that the speaker is *transported . . . in wonder, thanks, and praise*, that gratitude *glows within [his] thankful heart*, that *[his] cup* not simply is full but *run[s] o'er*, and that God's gifts number not just *ten thousand* but *ten thousand, thousand*. The prose half of Addison's article asserts that giving thanks comes naturally if we just open the faucet, and the poem proves this point by showing what flows forth when we turn the handle.

The successive stanzas of the poem do not form a progression of thought but can be enjoyed as "notes" on the subject of thanksgiving. Stanza 1 composes an imaginary setting in which we rise on wings to a high vantage point from which we can survey all of God's mercies. Stanza 2 employs a common rhetorical device called the *inexpressibility motif*, which is based on the premise "words fail me." In the next two stanzas, the poet shares original angles of vision on the subject of gratitude, and in the final stanza the poem enacts a familiar hymnic convention known as the *eschatological turn*, in which its focus shifts to the end of earthly history and the ushering in of eternity.

Two ingredients unify Addison's dizzying raptures into a coherent whole. One is the way in which he keeps the poem's focus single-mindedly on the motif of overflowing gratitude for God's lavish gifts. The second is the way in which the poem is continuously phrased as a prayer addressed to God.

The niche that this entry fills is that of a spiritual pep talk on gratitude. Whenever we start to feel that giving thanks is a burdensome duty, we can read Addison's essay and poem as a means of opening the gate for a walk in a pleasure park. ▪

It seems likely that Addison's poem took its point of departure from Psalm 89:1. Addison's poem begins with the prospect of surveying all God's mercies, and the psalmist begins in similar fashion by asserting, "I will sing of the mercies of the LORD for ever: with my mouth will I make known thy faithfulness to all generations" (KJV).

Adriaen van Ostade, *The Cottage Dooryard*, 1673

Family Thanksgivings in Puritan England

Oliver Heywood (1630–1702)

We had a solemn day of thanksgiving at my house for my wife's and son's recovery. My son Eliezer began. Mr. Dawson proceeded. I concluded with preaching and prayer. We feasted fifty persons and upwards, blessed be God.

Several months before my father died he was much affected with the sense of God's great goodness to him, and greatly drawn out in thankfulness to God in his prayers. Yea, he appointed several days of solemn thanksgiving on which he desired the help of Christian friends and neighbors, and was much enlarged upon those days.

On the Friday after April 27 we kept a day of thanksgiving for my brother and sister Whiteheads' recovery out of the fever, wherein God wonderfully helped my heart to reckon up his mercies.

God in his own due time did graciously recover my son John, so that upon Wednesday Jan. 30 I kept a day of thanksgiving and had several friends to help. It was a sweet day, and comfortably ordered, and a token for good.

UPON THURSDAY, NOV. 21, my wife and I rode to Bramley, and according to appointment we kept a day of solemn thanksgiving upon a family account. Oh, what a sweet day it was. In the close of it we enjoyed a sweet sealing . . . in the communing of saints.

ON MONDAY DEC. 16 we had a day of thanksgiving at William Clay's for his recovery. Blessed be the Lord, my heart was much affected.

ON DEC. 19 I WENT with my wife to Robert Ramsdens at Park Nook. There we celebrated a day of thanksgiving for his wife's delivery of two lively children, and for her recovery out of some other distempers. Oh, what a sweet day was it to my heart. Blessed be God for it.

ON THURSDAY, KEEPING A DAY of thanksgiving at Elias Hinchbulls, I preached a little, and on Friday we returned home and found all well, blessed be God. Oh for a thankful heart. . . . I spent a day of thanksgiving with Richard Mason . . . with good Mr. Pike for recovery out of sickness. ▪

THE FUNCTION OF THIS HISTORICAL entry is twofold. First, it provides exactly the right context for understanding the origins of the American Thanksgiving. But these passages from a Puritan pastor's diary rise above this historical context and open up promising avenues for expressing thanksgiving in our lives and our families.

One of the most endearing features of the English Puritans was their practice of holding family thanksgivings. Horton Davies, an authority on the English Puritans, explains that "Puritan families used to keep private days of thanksgiving. . . . Such days are not to be confused with national days of thanksgiving. . . . Any occasion in the life of a family that called for gratitude to God was celebrated as a day of thanksgiving." Examples include the delivery of a baby or the safe return of a family member after a hazardous journey. Such days, writes Davies, were "family festivals to which neighbors were invited" and at which the local minister was expected to conduct the family's devotions.

This is where the entries from Oliver Heywood's diary come into play. These snapshots from the life of a rural pastor give us a feel for what family thanksgivings were like. When Heywood was ejected from the pulpit for his Puritan convictions, he became an itinerant preacher, which explains the mobility that we sense from his diary entries. In a typical year, he presided at a dozen family thanksgivings.

What do we learn about these Puritan thanksgivings that can influence our own lives of gratitude? Although Heywood labels the days as being *solemn,* he also describes them as occasions during which people *feasted* and *celebrated.* Although their core group was usually a family, neighbors were also present. Yet some of Heywood's thanksgiving days were spent with just one or two acquaintances. In addition to these externalities are the responses that Heywood records after attending the thanksgivings. He speaks about being *much affected* and about *what a sweet day it was* and about how *God wonderfully helped [his] heart to reckon up his mercies.*

The takeaway from this entry is immense if we set ourselves to the task of unpacking it. We can follow the Puritan model of calling thanksgivings for the family only or for friends as well. Nothing is prescribed in terms of the day or hour chosen. What matters is that God's gifts are highlighted in a formal and potentially communal way, with an eye on participants' spiritual refreshment and renewed commitment to God. The possibilities keep expanding if we exercise our creativity in the matter. ▪

The case can be made that the Bible's original model for a family thanksgiving occurred on the night of the Passover in Egypt. The Passover was more than a thanksgiving ceremony, but it was not less. In brief, the family night unfolded as follows: "None of you shall go out of the door of his house until the morning. . . . You shall observe this rite as a statute. . . . And when you come to the land that the LORD will give you, as he has promised, you shall keep this service . . . , for [God] passed over the houses of the people of Israel in Egypt, when he struck the Egyptians but spared our houses" (Ex. 12:22, 24, 25, 27). The Israelites celebrated this event with gratitude.

Leopold Bruckner, Fresco in St. Nicholas
Church (Slovakia), late 1800s

Communal Thanksgivings in Puritan New England

William Bradford (1590–1657) and Edward Winslow (1595–1655)

Giving Thanks in Adversity, 1620

BEING THUS ARRIVED in a good harbor and brought safe to land, they fell upon their knees and blessed the God of heaven, who had brought them over the vast and furious ocean, and delivered them from all the perils and miseries thereof, again to set their feet on the firm and stable earth, their proper element. . . .

Being thus passed over the vast ocean . . . , they had now no friends to welcome them, nor inns to entertain or refresh their weather-beaten bodies, no houses or much less towns to repair to. . . . It was winter, and they that know the winters of that country know them to be sharp and violent, and subject to cruel and fierce storms, dangerous to travel to known places, much more to search an unknown coast. . . . What could now sustain them but the spirit of God and his grace? May not and ought not the children of these fathers rightly say: our fathers . . . came over this great ocean, and were ready to perish in this wilderness, but they cried unto the Lord, and he heard their voice, and looked on their adversity. Let them therefore praise the Lord, because he is good, and his mercies endure forever. . . . When they wandered in the desert . . . and found no city to dwell in, both hungry and thirsty, their soul was overwhelmed in them. Let them confess before the Lord his loving kindness, and his wonderful works before the sons of men.

The Original American Thanksgiving, 1621

OUR HARVEST BEING gotten in, our governor sent four men on fowling, that so we might after a more special manner rejoice together, after we had gathered the fruit of our labors; they four in one day killed as much fowl as, with a little help beside, served the company almost a week, at which time amongst other recreations, we exercised our arms, many of the Indians coming amongst us, and among the rest their greatest King Massasoit, with some ninety men, whom for three days we entertained and feasted. . . .

I never in my life remember a more seasonable year than we have here enjoyed, and . . . I make no question, but men might live as contented here as in any part of the world. For fish and fowl we have great abundance. . . . Here are grapes, white and red, and very sweet and strong also. . . . These things I thought good to let you understand, being the truth of things as near as I could experientally take knowledge of, and that you might on our behalf give God thanks who hath dealt so favorably with us. ◼

THESE ARE THE TWO MOST important "founding documents" of the American Thanksgiving. William Bradford, who was elected governor of Plymouth colony more than thirty times, wrote a history of the Pilgrims' journey on the *Mayflower* as well as their settlement in New England. The opening paragraph of the selection printed on the previous pages records the moment when the group first touched land in the New World. The picture of the Pilgrims falling to their knees and thanking God for their arrival is etched into our national consciousness and is nothing less than a real-life devotional.

The opening paragraph also paints a picture of the extreme hardships the Pilgrims endured. Nearly half of the original hundred died during the first winter. In this context, Governor Bradford expresses his trust in God's goodness. Giving thanks during adversity is his theme, and Bradford turns to Psalm 107 for the words with which to voice his gratitude to God.

The second passage is the definitive document on the origin of an American Thanksgiving. Its author, like William Bradford, came over on the *Mayflower*, was a leader during the early years of the colony, and wrote historical documents about his experiences. One of these is a 1622 pamphlet titled *Mourt's Relation: A Journal of the Beginning and Proceedings of the English Plantation Settled at Plymouth in New England*. It recounts in detail what happened during the first two years of the colony, including the festival that became the prototype of the American Thanksgiving. Winslow's account is part of a letter written to friends back in England.

There are no more famous and magical words surrounding the original New England thanksgiving than the ones that begin Winslow's account: *Our harvest being gotten in*. Contrary to the claims of debunkers of Winslow's account, who say that the Puritans and other Calvinists never celebrated and feasted, the picture that Winslow paints is entirely in keeping with what we know about the Puritans. William Bradshaw, a famous Puritan preacher, sounded the keynote when he claimed that it is "an illusion of Satan" that when people "devote themselves to the service of Jesus Christ . . . they must bid an everlasting farewell to all mirth and delight"; whereas, he argued, the truth "is the contrary: in the kingdom of Christ and in his house there is marrying and giving in marriage, drinking of wine, feasting, and rejoicing."

In the same vein, John Calvin wrote that "if we ponder to what end God created food, we shall find that he meant not only to provide for

previous: Raphaelle Peale,
Still Life with Cake, 1818

necessity but also for delight and good cheer." According to C. S. Lewis, the word *hilaritas*, or hilarity, captures the spirit of Calvin's phrase *good cheer*. Far from being an anomaly, the famous 1621 celebration was simply putting into practice what Puritan theory had always preached.

The documents printed above provide more than historical information. The spirit of thanksgiving and festivity that the Puritans exhibited is something that we can emulate—preeminently, but not only, on Thanksgiving Day. ■

The first New England thanksgiving calls to mind a moment in another nation's history two millennia earlier as recorded in the book of Nehemiah. After the public reading of God's law to the assembled remnant of Israelites, Nehemiah dismissed the people as follows: "'Go your way. Eat the fat and drink sweet wine and send portions to anyone who has nothing ready, for this day is holy to our Lord.' . . . And all the people went their way to eat and drink and to send portions and to make great rejoicing" (Neh. 8:10, 12).

Jennie Augusta Brownscombe,
Thanksgiving at Plymouth, 1925

Great Is Thy Faithfulness

Thomas Chisholm (1866–1960)

Great is thy faithfulness, O God my Father;
There is no shadow of turning with thee;
Thou changest not, thy compassions, they fail not;
As thou hast been, thou forever wilt be.

Summer and winter and springtime and harvest,
Sun, moon, and stars in their courses above
Join with all nature in manifold witness
To thy great faithfulness, mercy, and love.

Pardon for sin and a peace that endureth,
Thine own dear presence to cheer and to guide,
Strength for today and bright hope for tomorrow,
Blessings all mine, with ten thousand beside!

Refrain
Great is thy faithfulness!
Great is thy faithfulness!
Morning by morning new mercies I see;
All I have needed thy hand hath provided.
Great is thy faithfulness, Lord, unto me! ▪

ALTHOUGH THIS HYMN DOES NOT use the vocabulary of thanksgiving, it is in every way a thanksgiving text. From start to finish, it awakens our gratitude, which is surely the litmus test of a thanksgiving hymn. It expresses thanks to God in the format of prayer. Additionally, even though it uses the first-person *I* and *my* pronouns, when we sing the hymn in a congregational setting we experience it as a corporate testimony to God's faithfulness and our shared gratitude for it.

The backbone of a thanksgiving hymn or poem is a catalog of received blessings, accompanied by an acknowledgement that God is their source. "Great Is Thy Faithfulness" runs true to form in this regard—but with a surprise element. We usually think of God's gifts in terms of everyday provisions, but this poem of thanksgiving makes God himself the primary gift, which is then narrowed down to one of his specific divine attributes: his faithfulness, as announced in the opening line.

With this overarching theme in place, the poet follows the customary practice of making each stanza a variation on his main theme. Stanza 1 asserts, and implicitly expresses gratitude for, God's unchangeableness, but as it does so we are led to think specifically of God's *compassions* as changeless.

Stanza 2 is more complex. First the poet enlists the forces of nature as a *manifold witness* to the poem's theme. But he then expands that theme beyond God's *faithfulness* to include his *mercy and love*. More subtly, even though the evocative list of natural forces is ostensibly offered as a witness to God's beneficent character, we intuitively assimilate these elements of nature as gifts from God for which we are grateful in their own right.

Stanza 3 is an explosion of the main theme. Its first line introduces the specifically spiritual provisions of *pardon for sin* and *peace that endureth*. Then our gratitude extends to God's presence that both *cheer[s]* and *guide[s]*. The poet's strategy in this stanza is to encompass everything, and accordingly in the third line he refers to both *today* and *tomorrow*. The concluding line is the most expansive of all: it extends to all the blessings that have been named *with ten thousand beside*.

The refrain functions as a periodic punctuation mark and summary statement amid the fireworks of thanksgiving. Additionally, as we return to the thought that God's hand has provided *all [we] have needed*, it dawns on us that God's providence is the most obvious aspect of his faithfulness for which we are grateful.

previous: George Inness, *Sunrise*, 1887;
William Trost Richards, *Indian Summer*, 1875

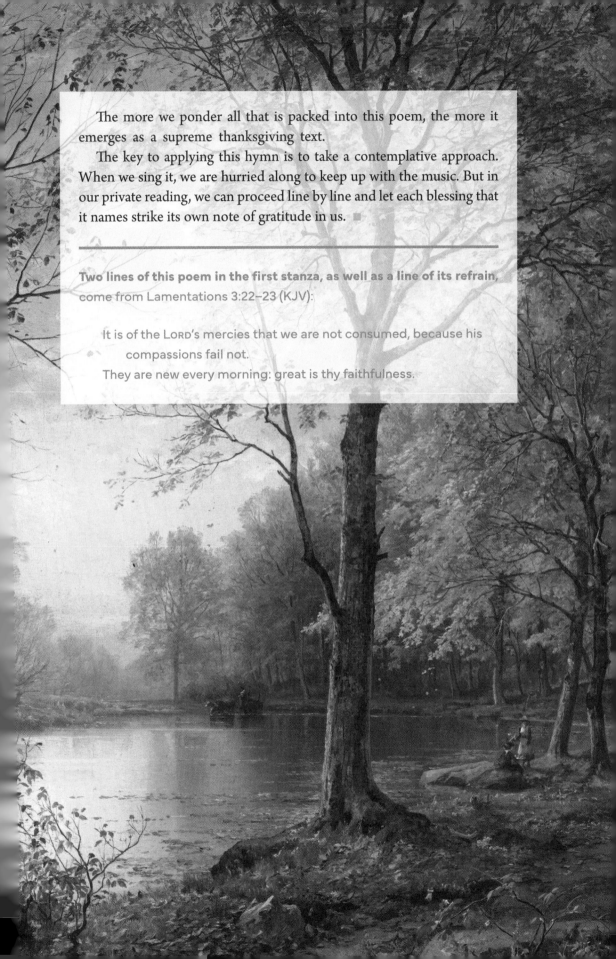

The more we ponder all that is packed into this poem, the more it emerges as a supreme thanksgiving text.

The key to applying this hymn is to take a contemplative approach. When we sing it, we are hurried along to keep up with the music. But in our private reading, we can proceed line by line and let each blessing that it names strike its own note of gratitude in us. ■

Two lines of this poem in the first stanza, as well as a line of its refrain, come from Lamentations 3:22–23 (KJV):

> It is of the LORD's mercies that we are not consumed, because his compassions fail not.
> They are new every morning: great is thy faithfulness.

Giving Thanks for Our Riches in Christ

EPHESIANS 1:3–14

Blessed be the God and Father of our Lord Jesus Christ,
    who has blessed us in Christ
    with every spiritual blessing in the heavenly places,
even as he chose us in him
    before the foundation of the world,
    that we should be holy and blameless before him.

In love he predestined us for adoption to himself
    as sons through Jesus Christ,
    according to the purpose of his will,
to the praise of his glorious grace,
    with which he has blessed us in the Beloved.

In him we have redemption through his blood,
    the forgiveness of our trespasses,
according to the riches of his grace,
    which he lavished upon us,
    in all wisdom and insight,

making known to us the mystery of his will,
   according to his purpose,
which he set forth in Christ
   as a plan for the fullness of time,
to unite all things in him,
   things in heaven and things on earth.

In him we have obtained an inheritance,
   having been predestined according to the purpose of him
   who works all things according to the counsel of his will,
so that we who were the first to hope in Christ
   might be to the praise of his glory.

In him you also, when you heard the word of truth,
   the gospel of your salvation,
   and believed in him,
were sealed with the promised Holy Spirit,
   who is the guarantee of our inheritance
   until we acquire possession of it,
   to the praise of his glory. ▪

THE DOORWAY TO ASSIMILATING THIS PASSAGE as a thanksgiving text is to understand the genre of the New Testament epistles. The biblical epistles follow a common format that consists of five elements: opening or salutation, thanksgiving, body of the letter, moral exhortations, and closing (final greetings and benediction). The authors of the epistles inherited this format from their surrounding Greco-Roman culture, yet the thanksgivings found in their letters have no precedent or parallel in the non-Christian world of the first century. They are unique. So even before we look closely at the content of an epistolary thanksgiving such as the one printed above, a rich vein of edification presents itself: we see there is something about belief in Christ that issues forth in exuberant, overflowing thanksgiving.

The epistolary thanksgiving in the book of Ephesians is representative of the form. The apostle Paul's opening formula *blessed be the God and Father* carries the force of *thanks be to God*. The first thing we note about the ensuing list of blessings for which Paul thanks God is that it is single-mindedly spiritual in nature. There is nothing here about a plentiful harvest or deliverance from physical danger or good health.

More specifically, the subject of this thanksgiving is the riches in Christ that every believer possesses. Paul's opening three lines set forth a thesis statement by speaking of how God *has blessed us in Christ with every*

Jaharis Byzantine
Lectionary, ca. 1100

spiritual blessing. As the passage then unfolds, the phrase *in him* appears six times, supplemented by the phrases *in the Beloved* and *in Christ*.

The template on which any thanksgiving poem is built is an inventory of blessings for which the recipient is grateful. These constitute the variations on the poem's main theme, and as we work our way through this particular epistolary thanksgiving, we can identify the following variations, all of which relate to the salvation of believers: being chosen by God from eternity, being adopted as children of Christ, receiving redemption and forgiveness of sins, receiving an inheritance for the future, and being sealed by the Holy Spirit.

Style contributes its part to the effect of this passage. Here Paul adopts what is called the *high style*, with long clauses and sentences that sweep us along and lift our emotions to an exalted realm. We get the impression that once the author has embarked on a train of thought, he cannot stop the onward rush of his ideas and feelings.

The takeaway of this passage is immense and falls primarily into two categories. First, this passage's inventory of spiritual blessings can help us to adjust our own attitudes. It is easy for us to dwell on temporal blessings when we think about thanksgiving, especially around the annual American holiday. This passage emphasizes the primacy of the spiritual. Second, the passage is about the spiritual riches that we possess *in Christ*, and so it intensifies our love for and devotion to the One who has saved us. ◼

This thanksgiving passage from Ephesians leads us to put into practice what is stated as a principle in 2 Corinthians 4:18: "We look not to the things that are seen but to the things that are unseen." It is for the unseen things described in Ephesians 1 that we are most thankful.

Medallion with Saint Paul from an
Icon Frame (Byzantine), ca. 1100

Amazing Grace

JOHN NEWTON (1725–1807)

Amazing grace! how sweet the sound,
That saved a wretch like me!
I once was lost but now am found,
Was blind but now I see.

'Twas grace that taught my heart to fear,
And grace my fears relieved;
How precious did that grace appear
The hour I first believed!

The Lord has promised good to me,
His word my hope secures;
He will my shield and portion be
As long as life endures.

Through many dangers, toils, and snares,
I have already come;
'Tis grace hath brought me safe thus far,
And grace will lead me home.

Yea, when this flesh and heart shall fail,
And mortal life shall cease,
I shall possess, within the veil,
A life of joy and peace. ▪

Tʜɪs ɪs ᴛʜᴇ ᴡᴏʀʟᴅ's ᴍᴏsᴛ ꜰᴀᴍᴏᴜs ʜʏᴍɴ, but is it a thanksgiving hymn? It is, and it serves as a test case for this anthology's claim that many familiar hymns can be experienced as thanksgiving hymns if we simply train ourselves to see them that way. We may do so by applying the usual criteria of what makes a text an expression of gratitude and thankfulness.

Before we do that, we should look at John Newton's hymn on its own terms. This is a hymn of personal testimony about the operation of God's grace in the life of a sinner who has been saved. In the poem, the speaker does what the Psalms command us to do: he remembers God's gracious acts and does not forget his benefits (see Ps. 103:2). The rehearsal is surely not informational in purpose but instead an exercise in gratitude. As we name the gifts we have received, we feel grateful for them.

With this general orientation setting our compass, we can proceed to analyze how "Amazing Grace" follows the content and format of a thanksgiving text. The backbone of a thanksgiving poem or hymn is a list of received blessings—one that has been implicitly formulated to explain why the author or speaker is grateful, and in what ways. That is what "Amazing Grace" does. The overriding blessing for which it expresses gratitude is God's grace. Under that umbrella, each stanza discusses a separate act of his grace. Stanza 1 puts "the big one" on the table: a person's once-for-all conversion. Stanza 2 relives, in a spirit of gratitude, the conviction of sin that leads to saving faith. Having thus looked back, the poem takes stock in stanza 3 of present assurance, and its next stanza covers similar territory by casting glances at the past, the present, and the future. The fifth stanza expresses gratitude for the eschatological hope of heaven.

The lesson to be learned from this hymn, and other familiar hymns like it, is that a poem does not need to use the vocabulary of thanksgiving in order be a thanksgiving text. What it needs to do is awaken our gratitude and prompt us to express our thankfulness. We can view this approach in terms of our completing a process of thanksgiving that the author enables us to perform by assembling the materials we need to do so.

Our application is twofold: (1) we can be on the alert for an untapped repository of thanksgiving hymns in our repertoire of familiar hymns, and (2) every time we sing or hear "Amazing Grace" we can remember that it is a great thanksgiving hymn as well as a testimonial hymn. ■

As we sing or read "Amazing Grace," we are led to feel grateful for God's totally transforming work of grace in our past, present, and future. In 1 Corinthians 1:4–7, Paul expresses a similar gratitude for the all-encompassing grace that he sees in the lives of fellow believers.

> I give thanks to my God always for you because of the grace of God that was given you in Christ Jesus, that in every way you were enriched in him in all speech and all knowledge—even as the testimony about Christ was confirmed among you—so that you are not lacking in any gift, as you wait for the revealing of our Lord Jesus Christ.

Isack van Ostade, *The Halt at the Inn*, 1645

Oh Give Thanks to the Lord

Psalm 107

Oh give thanks to the Lord, for he is good,
    for his steadfast love endures forever!
Let the redeemed of the Lord say so,
    whom he has redeemed from trouble
and gathered in from the lands,
    from the east and from the west,
    from the north and from the south.

Some wandered in desert wastes,
    finding no way to a city to dwell in;
hungry and thirsty,
    their soul fainted within them.
Then they cried to the Lord in their trouble,
    and he delivered them from their distress.
He led them by a straight way
    till they reached a city to dwell in.
Let them thank the Lord for his steadfast love,
    for his wondrous works to the children of man!
For he satisfies the longing soul,
    and the hungry soul he fills with good things.

Some sat in darkness and in the shadow of death,
    prisoners in affliction and in irons,
for they had rebelled against the words of God,
    and spurned the counsel of the Most High.
So he bowed their hearts down with hard labor;
    they fell down, with none to help.
Then they cried to the Lord in their trouble,
    and he delivered them from their distress.
He brought them out of darkness and the shadow of death,
    and burst their bonds apart.
Let them thank the Lord for his steadfast love,
    for his wondrous works to the children of man!
For he shatters the doors of bronze
    and cuts in two the bars of iron.

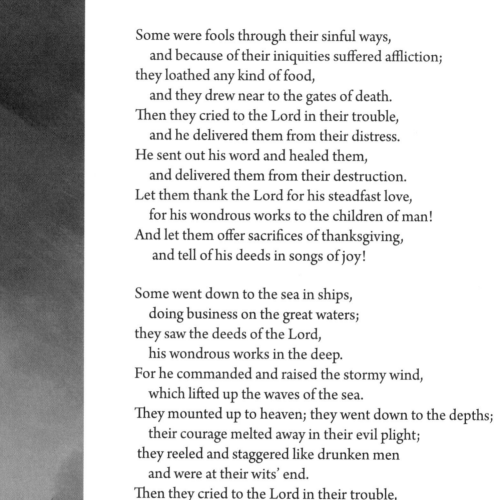

Some were fools through their sinful ways,
    and because of their iniquities suffered affliction;
they loathed any kind of food,
    and they drew near to the gates of death.
Then they cried to the Lord in their trouble,
    and he delivered them from their distress.
He sent out his word and healed them,
    and delivered them from their destruction.
Let them thank the Lord for his steadfast love,
    for his wondrous works to the children of man!
And let them offer sacrifices of thanksgiving,
    and tell of his deeds in songs of joy!

Some went down to the sea in ships,
    doing business on the great waters;
they saw the deeds of the Lord,
    his wondrous works in the deep.
For he commanded and raised the stormy wind,
    which lifted up the waves of the sea.
They mounted up to heaven; they went down to the depths;
    their courage melted away in their evil plight;
they reeled and staggered like drunken men
    and were at their wits' end.
Then they cried to the Lord in their trouble,
    and he delivered them from their distress.
He made the storm be still,
    and the waves of the sea were hushed.
Then they were glad that the waters were quiet,
    and he brought them to their desired haven.
Let them thank the Lord for his steadfast love,
    for his wondrous works to the children of man!
Let them extol him in the congregation of the people,
    and praise him in the assembly of the elders.

He turns rivers into a desert,
    springs of water into thirsty ground,
a fruitful land into a salty waste,
    because of the evil of its inhabitants.
He turns a desert into pools of water,
    a parched land into springs of water.
And there he lets the hungry dwell,
    and they establish a city to live in;
they sow fields and plant vineyards
    and get a fruitful yield.
By his blessing they multiply greatly,
    and he does not let their livestock diminish.

When they are diminished and brought low
    through oppression, evil, and sorrow,
he pours contempt on princes
    and makes them wander in trackless wastes;
but he raises up the needy out of affliction
    and makes their families like flocks.
The upright see it and are glad,
    and all wickedness shuts its mouth.

Whoever is wise, let him attend to these things;
    let them consider the steadfast love of the Lord. ■

Willem van de Velde the Younger, *Ships in a Gale*, 1660;
following: Jan Brueghel the Elder, *River Landscape*, 1607

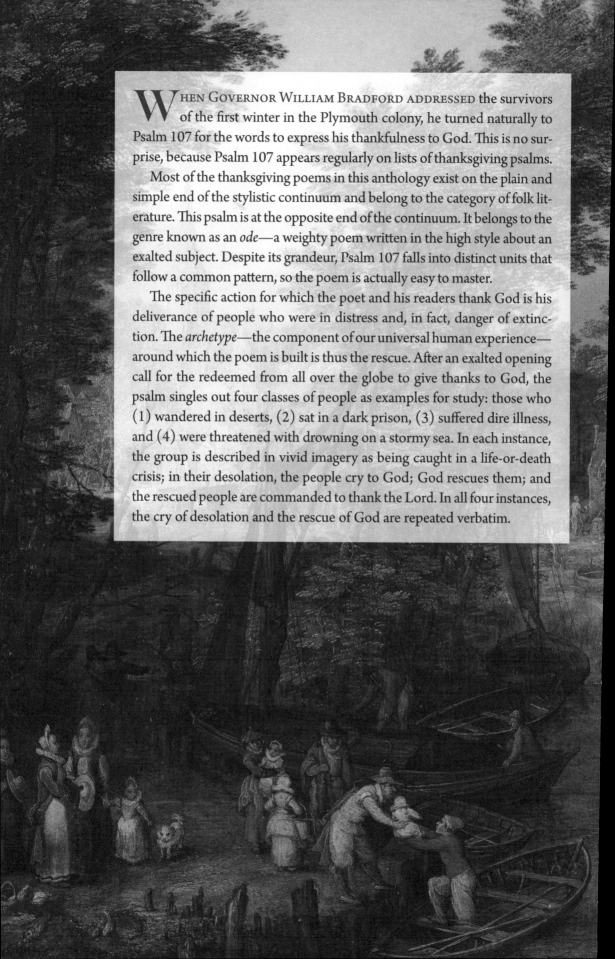

WHEN GOVERNOR WILLIAM BRADFORD ADDRESSED the survivors of the first winter in the Plymouth colony, he turned naturally to Psalm 107 for the words to express his thankfulness to God. This is no surprise, because Psalm 107 appears regularly on lists of thanksgiving psalms.

Most of the thanksgiving poems in this anthology exist on the plain and simple end of the stylistic continuum and belong to the category of folk literature. This psalm is at the opposite end of the continuum. It belongs to the genre known as an *ode*—a weighty poem written in the high style about an exalted subject. Despite its grandeur, Psalm 107 falls into distinct units that follow a common pattern, so the poem is actually easy to master.

The specific action for which the poet and his readers thank God is his deliverance of people who were in distress and, in fact, danger of extinction. The *archetype*—the component of our universal human experience—around which the poem is built is thus the rescue. After an exalted opening call for the redeemed from all over the globe to give thanks to God, the psalm singles out four classes of people as examples for study: those who (1) wandered in deserts, (2) sat in a dark prison, (3) suffered dire illness, and (4) were threatened with drowning on a stormy sea. In each instance, the group is described in vivid imagery as being caught in a life-or-death crisis; in their desolation, the people cry to God; God rescues them; and the rescued people are commanded to thank the Lord. In all four instances, the cry of desolation and the rescue of God are repeated verbatim.

The closing section of the psalm is a miscellaneous catalog of God's powerful acts, yet it still follows the same principle that has underlain the previous units: namely, God's reversing a condition. Here, however, God is described as bringing people either from undeserved prosperity to ruin or from deprivation to prosperity.

This psalm ranks specifically as a thanksgiving psalm because five times it commands us to *give thanks to the Lord* or *thank the Lord*. Our application of the poem comes when we see a metaphoric principle at work in the situations that it describes. At a figurative level, we all experience wanderings in desert wastes and imprisonment in dark places and illness that brings us near the gates of death and stormy winds that threaten to sink our ship. When God rescues us from these threats, we can obey the poem's commands by thanking him for his actions on our behalf. ∎

Psalm 107 is built around the archetypal rescue motif. This is no surprise, because the Bible is a huge anthology of rescue stories. Even its metanarrative, which Colossians 1:13–14 encapsulates, is a rescue story:

> He has rescued us from the power of darkness and transferred us into the kingdom of his beloved Son, in whom we have redemption, the forgiveness of sins. (NRSV)

This is the ultimate rescue—one worthy of our deepest thanksgiving.

You Whose Bounty Fills My Cup

JANE F. CREWDSON (1808–1863)

You whose bounty fills my cup
With every blessing meet,
I give you thanks for every drop—
The bitter and the sweet.

I thank you for the desert road,
And for the riverside;
For all your goodness has bestowed,
And all your grace denied.

I thank you for both smile and frown,
And for the gain and loss;
I thank you for the future crown,
And for the present cross.

I thank you for the wing of love
That stirred my worldly nest,
And for the stormy clouds that drove
The flutterer to your breast.

I thank you for the glad increase,
And for the waning joy,
And for this strange, this settled peace,
That nothing can destroy. ■

Tʜᴇ sᴛʀɪᴋɪɴɢ ᴏᴘᴇɴɪɴɢ ʟɪɴᴇ ᴏғ Jane Crewdson's poem serves as a welcome invitation for us to undertake the journey that she has prepared. The line's direct address to God introduces the quality of a con-

versation with a friend that persists throughout the poem. The word *bounty* awakens desire and longing, identifying something that everyone understands and wants. And the image of a cup that is full to overflowing reaches back to one of the most evocative statements in the Bible: David's declaration that his "cup overflows" (Ps. 23:5).

The poem possesses a quiet simplicity, befitting the work of an author who lived in obscurity in Victorian England. After its opening stanza announces the poem's main idea, every subsequent stanza begins with the repeated formula *I thank you for*. The poem then follows the standard convention of a thanksgiving poem by listing things *for which* the poet is thankful.

But at this point the poem springs surprises on us. The pattern of repetition we have just noted is balanced by a rhetoric of contrast. Every stanza introduces a contrast between experiences that we consider desirable and ones that we consider undesirable and try to avoid. Surprisingly, the poem expresses equal gratitude for both categories of experience.

As we think about this, we can see that we need to add a further, more complex category to the simple rhetoric of conversation, repetition, and contrast noted in the preceding paragraphs. It is called *paradox*. A paradox is an apparent contradiction that, on reflection, can be seen to express truth. In other words, it needs to be resolved. In the case of this poem, we infer that everything that God sends is part of his providential working in our lives and can therefore be received as a blessing. The poem does not spell out how this is true, so it is up to us to ponder the matter and come to the right conclusions on our own.

Beaker (England), 1690/91; Cup (Iraq), 9th–10th century; Cup with geometric decoration (Nubia), 1st–3rd century

At this point the poet's biography provides a helpful context. Crewdson suffered from fragile health throughout her life. During her later years, which is when she produced the poetry for which she is known, she became a bedridden invalid. Her husband recorded that visitors resorted to her room to receive refreshment of spirit. A biographer offers the summary statement that "she truly learned in suffering what she taught in song."

The takeaway from this poem is the corrective it offers to conventional thinking about gratitude. We ourselves would not ordinarily include the negative experiences named in the poem in our list of things for which we are grateful. The poem thus prompts us to reconsider how we think about adversity and deprivation. ■

Underlying Crewdson's poem is the idea that suffering can produce virtues, and, in Romans 5:3–5, Paul concurs. Thus we have a reason to be grateful even for suffering.

> We rejoice in our sufferings, knowing that suffering produces endurance, and endurance produces character, and character produces hope, and hope does not put us to shame, because God's love has been poured into our hearts through the Holy Spirit who has been given to us.

John Frederick Peto,
Breakfast, ca. 1890s

For the Beauty of the Earth

Folliott S. Pierpoint (1835–1917)

For the beauty of the earth,
For the glory of the skies,
For the love which from our birth
Over and around us lies,
  Lord of all to thee we raise
  This our hymn of grateful praise.

For the beauty of each hour
Of the day and of the night,
Hill and vale and tree and flow'r,
Sun and moon and stars of light.
  Lord of all to thee we raise
  This our hymn of grateful praise.

For the joy of human love,
Brother, sister, parent, child,
Friends on earth, and friends above,
For all gentle thoughts and mild,
  Lord of all to thee we raise
  This our hymn of grateful praise.

For yourself, best gift divine,
To the world so freely giv'n,
Agent of God's grand design:
Peace on earth and joy in heav'n,
  Lord of all to thee we raise
  This our hymn of grateful praise.

THIS HYMN IS ON THE "short list" of Thanksgiving hymns, being one of five that are most regularly sung at Thanksgiving church services. One reason is the hymn's comprehensiveness. Its opening obscures this, because instead of following poets' and hymnwriters' usual practice of beginning with a broad thematic statement that introduces everything that follows, the author of this hymnic poem begins with a specific blessing: *the beauty of the earth*. But the poem as a whole covers a vast spectrum by giving thanks for beauty and love in stanza 1, the physical world of nature in stanza 2, the human world of relationships in stanza 3, and the spiritual world, of which God is the center, in stanza 4.

A second reason for the hymn's popularity at Thanksgiving, in addition to its comprehensiveness, is its winsome simplicity that makes it immediately accessible to everyone. Its simple verse form, the *quatrain*, comes from the folk tradition of English poetry and consists of a four-line stanza that rhymes *abab*. Rather than elaborating on the list in each stanza, the

poet ends each stanza with a two-line refrain that keeps returning us to the main idea of the hymn. In the same vein, the repetition of the formula *for*, followed by the naming of benefits for which the poet is grateful, shows that the poem is structured as a simple catalog of blessings, which can be easily assimilated in either singing or reading.

The surface simplicity that we have noted within the hymn is balanced by features of the grand. For example, each stanza consists of a single long sentence. And not only that—the sentences adhere to what is known as *suspended sentence structure*. First, this structure inverts normal word order in such a way that a sentence's main clause comes last instead of first. Second, as the subordinate clauses keep piling up, they require us to keep reading or singing before the idea of the sentence is completed. A mild tension builds up as we are kept wondering when and how the sentence will end. This way of handling sentence structure belongs to what is called

Martin Johnson Heade, *New-buryport Meadows*, ca. 1876–81

the *exalted* or *high style*, a style that fits the subject of thanking God for his blessings bestowed.

There is an additional way this hymn uses phraseology to elevate its style and express exuberance. It enumerates the specific ingredients of a subject instead of simply naming the subject's overall category. In the first stanza, for example, *the beauty of the earth* telescopes outward to include *the glory of the skies*, and the love we have known is not only traced all the way back to *our birth* but extended to the love that lies *over and around us* at every moment. In the second stanza, no fewer than nine forces of nature are named: *day, night, hill, vale, tree, flower, sun, moon, stars.* And so forth.

We can apply this hymn to our lives by taking time to meditate on our personal experiences of the categories it names. For example, what love have we ourselves known from our births and now experience all around us (stanza 1)? What encounters have we had with nature that have prompted our gratitude to God (stanza 2)? Who are the family members and friends we can claim as a source of blessing (stanza 3)? ■

Folliott Pierpoint's hymn is a natural fit with the psalms of thanksgiving. Psalm 105:1 is an example: "Oh give thanks to the Lord; call upon his name; make known his deeds among the peoples!"

Shaikh Zain al-Din, *An Orange-Headed Ground Thrush and a Death's-Head Moth on a Purple Ebony Orchid Branch*, 1778

Natural and Gracious Gratitude

Jonathan Edwards (1703–1758)

GRATITUDE IS ONE of the natural affections of the human soul. . . . [Natural] gratitude is an affection people have towards others for loving them, or gratifying them. . . . We see in innumerable instances that mere nature is sufficient to excite gratitude in people or to affect their hearts with thankfulness to others for kindnesses received. . . . And as people, from mere nature, may be thus affected towards fellow humans, so they may towards God. . . .

But these things by no means imply that all gratitude to God is a mere natural thing, and that there is no such thing as a spiritual gratitude, which is a holy and divine affection. They imply no more than that there is a gratitude that is *merely natural,* and that when persons have affections towards God only or primarily for *benefits* received, their affection is only the exercise of natural gratitude. There is [also] such a thing as a gracious gratitude, which greatly differs from all that gratitude that natural people experience.

True gratitude, or thankfulness to God for his kindness to us, arises from a foundation, laid before, of love to God for what he is in *himself,* whereas a natural gratitude has no such antecedent foundation. The gracious stirrings of grateful affection to God for kindness received always are from a stock of love already in the heart, established in the first place on other grounds, namely, God's own excellency; and hence the affections are disposed to flow out on occasions of God's kindness. The saint having seen the glory of God, and his heart overcome by it, and captivated into a supreme love to him on that account, his heart hereby becomes tender, and easily affected with kindness received. . . . Self-love is not excluded from a gracious gratitude; the saints love God *for his kindness to them.* . . . But something else is *included*; another love prepares the way, and lays the foundation for these grateful affections.

In a gracious gratitude, people are affected with the attribute of God's goodness and free grace, not only as they are concerned in it, or as it affects their interest, but as a part of the glory and beauty of God's nature. That wonderful and unparalleled grace of God which is manifested in the work of redemption, and shines forth in the face of Jesus Christ, is infinitely glorious in itself. . . . This would be glorious, whether it were exercised towards us or no, and the saint who exercises a gracious thankfulness for it sees it to be so, and delights in it as such. . . . Self-love here assists as a handmaid, being subservient to higher principles, to lead forth the mind to contemplation, and to heighten joy and love. . . .

A holy thankfulness to God . . . was laid in the heart before, in love to God for his excellency in himself; that makes the heart tender and susceptible of such impressions from his goodness to us. Nor is our own interest, or the benefits we have received, the only or the chief objective ground of the present exercises of the affection, but rather God's goodness, as part of the beauty of his nature. ■

Jonathan Edwards is one of the most important religious figures in American history. Influential in his own lifetime, and a highly visible public figure, he even served briefly as president of Princeton University before his death. He was at the center of the religious controversies of his day, so we can say with confidence that his views on gratitude and ingratitude were field-tested in the crucible of life. In the passage from which this entry has been drawn, Edwards offers the opinion that because gratitude is "a natural principle, it renders ingratitude so much the more vile and heinous," because it "suppresses the better principles of human nature." Edwards's insight here is important: to understand gratitude as a spiritual virtue, we also need to consider its opposite.

Because Edwards was a philosophical theologian, it is not surprising that in the passage printed above he takes an analytic approach to the subject of gratitude. It is as though he invites us to join him for a fireside tutorial on the nature of gratitude, with the goal of leading us to understand it better. The rhetorical device that Edwards uses is *contrast*. From start to finish, he contrasts two kinds of gratitude. One is the gratitude that all people, at their best, spontaneously exhibit. It belongs to the ethical category of natural virtue. Natural gratitude, whether it is expressed toward people or toward God, is a response to a benefit that has been given and received. Edwards wants us to know that spiritual virtue is different from that—it is something higher. It is gratitude that a believer always feels toward God for his saving grace and his beauty of character.

Giovanni Larciani , *Sacrifice of Noah (?)*, date uncertain

How might these two types of gratitude relate to each other? Edwards's discussion clarifies their relation admirably. We note first that he does not disparage the natural gratitude that is expressed by both unbelievers and believers. Gratitude for gifts received is an expression of human nature, as God created it and desires it to be. We should applaud such gratitude whenever we see it. But of course there is another component to spiritual gratitude that is expressed to God, and Edwards helpfully describes the characteristics of this higher form of gratitude.

Our spiritual gratitude is independent of any benefit we have received and is instead rooted in our experience of God himself and his saving work. To understand this is to open a door to understanding the claims of numerous believers that we can be thankful even when we experience deprivation or suffering. If we think about the matter as Edwards invites us to, we can begin to see a logic to being grateful in the absence of earthly benefits.

Despite Edwards's philosophical bent, his writings possess an undertow of lyric emotionalism whenever he discusses the glory and beauty of God. The vocabulary within the passage is afire with such expressions as the *excellency* of God and the believer's *affections [being] disposed to flow out on occasions of God's kindness* and *the glory and beauty of God's nature* that *shines forth in the face of Jesus Christ*. While engaging our minds, this passage also gives us a spiritual uplift.

The takeaway from the passage is a clarification of the two types of gratitude that we ourselves feel and that we also see in others. Fresh understanding motivates us to pursue spiritual gratitude in our daily lives. ▪

Edwards believes that we will be on the right track to live a life of gratitude if we set our compass in the direction of being grateful, above all, for God's love for us. As Paul writes in Ephesians 2, "God, being rich in mercy, because of the great love with which he loved us, even when we were dead in our trespasses, made us alive together with Christ" (vv. 4–5). This is the foundation for our thankfulness in lesser matters.

Anders Zorn, *At Prayer*, 1912; following: Yokoi Kinkoku, *Catching Fish under Willows in the Rain (Summer)*, ca. 1800

Thanksgivings on Specific Occasions

BOOK OF COMMON PRAYER

Thanksgiving for Rain

O GOD OUR HEAVENLY FATHER, who by thy gracious providence dost cause the former and the latter rain to descend upon the earth, that it may bring forth fruit for the use of man, we give thee humble thanks that it hath pleased thee in our great necessity to send us at the last a joyful rain upon thine inheritance, and to refresh it when it was dry, to the great comfort of us thy unworthy servants, and to the glory of thy holy name through thy mercies in Jesus Christ our Lord. Amen.

Thanksgiving for Abundant Provision

O MOST MERCIFUL FATHER, who of thy gracious goodness hast heard the devout prayers of thy church, and turned our scarcity into plenty, we give thee humble thanks for this thy special bounty, beseeching thee to continue thy loving-kindness unto us, that our land may yield us her fruits of increase to thy glory and our comfort through Jesus Christ our Lord. Amen.

Thanksgiving for Deliverance from Illness

O LORD GOD, . . . seeing it hath pleased thee of thy tender mercy . . . to assuage the contagious sickness wherewith we lately have been sore afflicted, and to restore the voice of joy and health into our dwellings, we offer unto thy divine majesty the sacrifice of praise and thanksgiving, lauding and magnifying thy glorious name for thy preservation and providence over us, through Jesus Christ our Lord. Amen.

Thanksgiving for a Mother's Safe Delivery of a Child

FORASMUCH AS IT hath pleased Almighty God of his goodness to give you safe deliverance, and hath preserved you in the great danger of child-birth, you shall give hearty thanks unto God, and say, . . .

> Gracious is the Lord, and righteous,
>   yea, our God is merciful;
> the Lord preserveth the simple;
>   I was in misery, and he helped me. (Ps. 116:5–6)

Thanksgiving at a Communion Service

ALMIGHTY AND EVERLASTING GOD, we most heartily thank thee, for . . . feeding us, who have duly received these holy mysteries, with the spiritual food of the most precious body and blood of thy Son our Savior Jesus Christ, and assuring us thereby of thy favor and goodness toward us, and that we are very members incorporate in the mystical body of thy Son, which is the blessed company of all faithful people, and are also heirs through hope of thy everlasting kingdom, by the merits of the most precious death and passion of thy dear Son. ■

A<small>N EARLIER ENTRY IN THIS</small> anthology presents general thanksgivings from the Book of Common Prayer. Those thanksgivings are called *general* because they apply to life as we live it continuously—they are prayers of gratitude for work, for example, or family. The technical designation for the genre of the passages that are printed in this entry is *occasional*, meaning that they express gratitude for specific occasions. The division of thanksgivings into these two categories is itself helpful as we think about thanksgiving.

By virtue of appearing in the Book of Common Prayer, the occasional thanksgivings printed in this section are intended for congregational prayer in a group setting. John Calvin was of the opinion that congregational thanksgiving is essential, writing that "the faithful should come into [God's] sanctuary" to give thanks and, further, that "the design of public and solemn thanksgiving is that the faithful . . . may encourage one another." This does not mean that we cannot as individuals read public expressions of thanks such as those printed above. The point is that we should, in the words of the prayer book's communion service, "at all times and in all places give thanks."

The spiritual effect of these passages from the Book of Common Prayer is enhanced by the beauty of their language and *syntax* (sentence structure). The long, flowing sentences carry us along and elevate us. The rhythm of the phrases creates what is known technically as *cadence*—the wavelike rise and fall of language that is pleasing in its regularity. As for the words, they are exalted and beautiful, exemplifying the claim of the Greek playwright Aristophanes that "high thoughts must have high language."

If we ask what the passage illuminates about thanksgiving, the most immediate answer is that its prayers keep our focus on God. They are

previous: Jean Honoré Fragonard, *Roman Interior*, ca. 1760; *Girls at Prayer in Church*, 1800s addressed to God because he is the source of the specific blessings that they keep in view. But the actual content of the prayers is likewise developed in such a way that every detail is ascribed to God's benevolent providence.

Entries in this anthology that consist of prayers lead naturally to the question of how we can best assimilate them as private devotionals. We can read them as prayers, first of all, allowing the authors to be our representatives as they say what we too want to say to God—only saying it better than we can. Additionally, as we ponder their individual assertions, they can become for us a meditation on the spiritual life—one that emphasizes God's providential governance of our lives on extraordinary occasions. And as their elevated thoughts and beautiful language have their combined effect, we find that they "set the affections in right tune," as John Milton phrased it.

Our applications are multiple. We can seize occasions of public thanksgiving that present themselves to us. At a more private level, we can take note of specific and perhaps extraordinary blessings from God and can express our formal thanks accordingly. And we can value beauty of expression in our worship services, such as that provided by the Book of Common Prayer. ▪

Occasional thanksgivings such as those in this entry owe their being to the doctrine of providence. We see a similar acknowledgment of God's providence combined with his followers' thanks in Psalm 145:9–10:

> The LORD is good to all,
>   and his mercy is over all that he has made.
>
> All your works shall give thanks to you, O LORD,
>   and all your saints shall bless you!

Célestin François Nanteuil,
Mary and Elizabeth, 1873

Giving Thanks for the Greatest Gift

Mary and Zechariah

The Magnificat

My soul magnifies the Lord,
    and my spirit rejoices in God my Savior,
for he has looked on the humble estate of his servant.
    For behold, from now on all generations will call me blessed;
for he who is mighty has done great things for me,
    and holy is his name.
And his mercy is for those who fear him
    from generation to generation.
He has shown strength with his arm;
    he has scattered the proud in the thoughts of their hearts;
he has brought down the mighty from their thrones
    and exalted those of humble estate;
he has filled the hungry with good things,
    and the rich he has sent away empty.
He has helped his servant Israel,
    in remembrance of his mercy,
as he spoke to our fathers,
    to Abraham and to his offspring forever.

The Song of Zechariah

Blessed be the Lord God of Israel,
    for he has visited and redeemed his people
and has raised up a horn of salvation for us
    in the house of his servant David,
as he spoke by the mouth of his holy prophets from of old,
that we should be saved from our enemies
    and from the hand of all who hate us;
to show the mercy promised to our fathers
    and to remember his holy covenant,
the oath that he swore to our father Abraham, to grant us
    that we, being delivered from the hand of our enemies,
might serve him without fear,
    in holiness and righteousness before him all our days. ▪

A N EARLIER ENTRY COLLECTED FIVE narrative moments in which Old Testament figures responded with immediate thanksgiving to momentous blessings from God. This selection presents two more such examples. One is Mary's spontaneous response to the annunciation from the angel Gabriel that she would bear the Christ child. The second is Zechariah's response to Jesus' promised coming, which Zechariah voiced after his son, John, was born and he regained his ability to speak. These two poems are the first thanksgiving poems of the Christian era, uttered by actual participants in the events of Jesus' birth. A good framework for assimilating them is to view them as answers to the implied question "Why should we be thankful for the coming of Christ to earth?"

Mary begins by taking stock of her own situation. She gives thanks because God *has done great things for [her]*. She is of *humble estate*—without an inherent claim to being singled out for such a privileged position that *all generations will call [her] blessed*. From this we can learn that it is appropriate for us to be ecstatically grateful for the blessings God bestows on us individually. We can also view Mary as our representative, since we too are persons of *humble estate* for whom God *has done great things*. All believers can thank God, as Mary does, for being singled out for the blessing of redemption.

After the introspection of the first six lines of her prayer, Mary's gratitude expands to encompass the past, present, and future. The foundation for her effusion of gratitude is the messianic promises that God had made in the past. Through the birth of Jesus, God has remembered to show the mercy he promised to Abraham. Mary is also grateful for the blessings of the present, and the keynote of her prayer is that the coming of the Messiah is the beginning of a great revolution in human history. It is a reversal of human values—one in which God raises up the needy and puts down the privileged. Salvation is for those who recognize their spiritual poverty, as Jesus himself confirmed in his beatitude "Blessed are the poor in spirit, for theirs is the kingdom of heaven" (Matt. 5:3). And this new messianic age will last *forever*, as Mary signals in her final word.

Zechariah's thanksgiving poem carries on from where Mary's ends. Zechariah makes his focus more specific than Mary's generalized picture of reversal. He expresses gratitude for the way in which God *has visited and redeemed his people*.

Francesco Granacci, *Scenes from the Life of Saint John the Baptist*, ca. 1506–7

This *salvation* is not only a revolution but also a deliverance for God's people *from the hand of our enemies*, of whom the ultimate examples are surely Satan, sin, and death. Those who have been thus saved through Christ are enabled to *serve him . . . in holiness and righteousness*.

We should allow these inspired words of Mary and Zechariah to move us to the same gratitude that they felt, and for the same reasons: for the favor that we have each received from God and for his great acts of redemption, which have revolutionized human history and delivered those who believe in Christ. ■

The scope of these thanksgiving poems is nothing less than salvation history—the unifying story of the Bible. Both Mary and Zechariah refer to Abraham as the fountainhead of God's promise to redeem the human race, as recorded in Genesis 12:2–3: "I will make of you a great nation, and I will bless you and make your name great, so that you will be a blessing . . . , and in you all the families of the earth shall be blessed."

Henry Ossawa Tanner, *The Annunciation*, 1898

Why We Need a National Thanksgiving Day

SARAH HALE (1788–1879)

OH, PRAISE THE LORD, for he is good, and his mercy endureth forever.

Amidst all the agitations that stir the minds of men and cause the hearts of women to tremble in fear and sorrow, among all the woes generated by human passions and human sins, the mercy of the Lord is over his children. It is the King of Heaven who gives us, year by year, the kindly fruits of the earth, and prepares our bread in due season. . . . We must acknowledge that the goodness of God has not failed. Shall we not, then, lay aside . . . our worldly cares, toils, and pursuits on one day in the year, devoting it to a public Thanksgiving for all the good gifts God has bestowed on us and on all the earth? . . .

All nations are members of one brotherhood, under the fostering care of the one beneficent Father of humanity. What could do more to arouse and preserve the fraternal feelings that should exist, especially among the nations of Christendom, than the establishment and universal observance of one general Christian Festival of Thanksgiving, on the same day of the year, throughout those nations? All sects and creeds who take the Bible as their rule of faith and morals could unite in such a festival. The Jews, also, who find the direct command for a feast at the ingathering of harvest, would gladly join in this Thanksgiving. . . .

There is something cheering and delightful in the idea of a day of universal thanksgiving . . . when all hearts are united in one sentiment of gratitude to the Divine Father of humanity. . . .

Who can estimate the benefits and blessings which may flow from the faithful observance of this happy Festival? . . .

This great national and domestic festival will be celebrated with happy recollections and cheerful hopes, and with grateful and softened hearts.

Let us all, with devout thankfulness to the beneficent Giver of all good gifts, do our best to make this coming Thanksgiving Day a foretaste of that happy period of "peace on earth and goodwill among men," in which all wrongs and sufferings from evil are to dissolve like shadows before the noonday sun, in the righteousness and goodness which will crown the glorious reign of Christ on earth.

Thanksgiving Hymn

Our Father, to thy throne our thoughts ascend
  In grateful symphony of thanks and praise,
For all the mercies that our steps attend,
  The smiles that bless, the hopes that cheer our days.
For all the bounties of the fruitful sod,
We give thee thanks, our Father and our God.

We thank thee for the guiding radiance shed
  Along the way wherein we journey here;
The faith that smooths the loftiest steep we tread;
  The hope that lights us through the vale most drear;
The love unequalled, shown by Him who died
  That we might live, who lives that we may rise
Through death to follow him, the Crucified,
  Redeemer and Exemplar, to the skies.
We mark the shining path our Leader trod,
And give thee thanks, our Father and our God. ▪

SARAH HALE WAS FAMOUS IN her time as an advocate for women's education, author of an antislavery novel, and editor of a prominent ladies' magazine. This combination made her one of the most important influences on the American life of her day. As a small confirmation of this, the first speech that Thomas Edison recorded on his newly invented phonograph was Hale's nursery rhyme "Mary Had a Little Lamb."

Hale is now known as the mother of Thanksgiving because she advocated for it in a series of annual editorials and letters that she wrote to five American presidents over a span of four decades, starting in 1837. During the early years of Hale's efforts, individual states in New England celebrated their own Thanksgiving days according to their own timetables. Hale's dream of a national Thanksgiving was finally realized in 1863 when

Eastman Johnson, *Feeding the Turkey*, ca. 1872–80;
following: Carducius Plantagenet Ream, *Blackberries Spilling from Tin Cup*, no date

Abraham Lincoln was persuaded by a letter from her to support legislation for a nation-wide holiday.

This entry's reading consists of excerpts from two of Hale's editorials. Their edification emerges as we analyze what Hale believed a national day of Thanksgiving could achieve individually and corporately. The first thing we notice is how much religious fervor permeates Hale's vision. She describes what she calls a Christian Festival of Thanksgiving. The content and nature of this holiday is solidly rooted in the Bible, and her goal is for it to be spent in outpouring thanks to God. Hale's proposal is not simply broadly religious but very specifically related to the Christian God and the saving work of Christ.

Intertwined with this dimension of personal piety and corporate Christian devotion is a civil and national element. Hale is rapturous about the blessings that could come to the United States (and to worldwide Christendom—though that part of her vision was never realized) through such a nationwide holiday. Among the social blessings that Hale lists as potential results are the following: a halt to the toil and anxiety of everyday life, time to reflect on the provisions we have received, festivity, and goodwill among citizens.

Hale included thanksgiving poems in some of her annual editorials, and the one that was attached to her 1864 editorial, printed in this entry, would be right at home in a Christian worship service. It is a prayer addressed to God the Father. Following the usual format of a thanksgiving poem, it lists the blessings for which its author and readers are grateful. This list ends with the redemption that Jesus purchased and the example that he gave us to follow.

Sarah Hale's picture of national thanksgiving gives us a model that, if put into practice, will ensure that our annual Thanksgiving celebration is a truly religious experience. Should we drift into a secular attitude about Thanksgiving Day, we can allow Hale's vision to serve as a corrective. ▪

Throughout her editorials, Hale referenced the Old Testament thanksgiving festivals as a model and warrant for a national day of thanksgiving. One of these is the Feast of Ingathering held at the end of Israel's annual harvest of grains and fruits. It was instituted in Exodus 23:16: "You shall keep the Feast of Ingathering at the end of the year, when you gather in from the field the fruit of your labor."

Thanksgiving Proclamation

ABRAHAM LINCOLN (1809–1865)

IT HAS PLEASED Almighty God to prolong our national life another year, defending us with His guardian care against unfriendly designs from abroad and vouchsafing to us in His mercy many and signal victories over the enemy, who is of our own household. It has also pleased our Heavenly Father to favor as well our citizens in their homes as our soldiers in their camps and our sailors on the rivers and seas with unusual health. He has largely augmented our free population by emancipation and by immigration, while He has opened to us new sources of wealth and has crowned the labor of our workingmen in every department of industry with abundant rewards.

Moreover, He has been pleased to animate and inspire our minds and hearts with fortitude, courage, and resolution sufficient for the great trial of civil war into which we have been brought by our adherence as a nation to the cause of freedom and humanity, and to afford to us reasonable hopes of an ultimate and happy deliverance from all our dangers and afflictions:

Now, therefore, I, Abraham Lincoln, President of the United States, do hereby appoint and set apart the last Thursday in November next as a day which I desire to be observed by all my fellow-citizens, wherever they may then be, as a day of thanksgiving and praise to Almighty God, the beneficent Creator and Ruler of the Universe.

And I do further recommend to my fellow-citizens aforesaid that on that occasion they do reverently humble themselves in the dust and from thence offer up penitent and fervent prayers and supplications to the Great Disposer of Events for a return of the inestimable blessings of peace, union, and harmony throughout the land which it has pleased Him to assign as a dwelling place for ourselves and for our posterity throughout all generations.

In testimony whereof I have hereunto set my hand and caused the seal of the United States to be affixed. Done at the city of Washington, this 20th day of October, A.D. 1864. ABRAHAM LINCOLN.

MANY FAMOUS EVENTS AND DOCUMENTS play their part in the history of the American Thanksgiving, but towering above all the others are Edward Winslow's account of the Pilgrims' three-day celebration in 1621 and Abraham Lincoln's 1864 presidential proclamation. It is a little-known fact that Lincoln was not the first American president to call the nation to a day of thanksgiving. In 1789, George Washington designated for "the people of the United States a day of public thanksgiving," and he appointed the last Thursday of November for this purpose. Lincoln followed Washington's lead in virtually every detail, including the general content of his proclamation.

Two more immediate influences shaped Lincoln's famous proclamation. One is the tireless efforts of Sarah Hale noted in the previous entry. In addition to the annual editorials that Hale wrote to keep her crusade alive, she sent a letter to President Lincoln in 1863 that urged him to make Thanksgiving a "national and fixed union festival." One year later, he did just that. Second, as Lincoln elaborates in the first half of his declaration, there was the national crisis of the moment—the height of the Civil War. To call the nation to thanksgiving at such a moment displayed faith in the goodness of God despite adversity as well as courage to carry on and reject defeatism.

The rhetoric and logic of Lincoln's proclamation deserve to be analyzed and praised just as his 1863 Gettysburg Address has been. The structure of the proclamation follows a firm logic. First, Lincoln surveys the national blessings of the preceding year. Thanksgiving is always preceded by a feeling of gratitude, which in turn is rooted in an awareness of benefits that have been granted and received. On the basis of the national blessings thus enumerated, Lincoln *therefore*, in his official role as *President of the United States*, does *appoint and set apart the last Thursday in November* to be a day of thanksgiving. Everything about this declaration is official and exalted, which elevates our spirits progressively as its sentences unfold.

The religious content of the declaration is likewise elevating. The doctrinal underpinning of thanksgiving is always

previous: Winslow Homer, *The Veteran in a New Field*, 1865
Daniel Chester French, *Abraham Lincoln*, modeled 1912

divine providence, and this proclamation fully evidences that in two ways. One is its catalog of benefits that God had sent to the nation, as already noted. The other is the string of *epithets* (titles) that it uses for God, which keep his sovereign government of events in view: *Almighty God, beneficent Creator and Ruler of the Universe, the Great Disposer of Events.* We do not automatically link thanksgiving with penitence, but Lincoln does— he calls on citizens to *humble themselves in the dust and from thence offer up penitent and fervent prayers and supplications* for the return of pre-war peace and union.

This proclamation would not have the effect that it does if it did not possess verbal and stylistic beauty. Its sentences are long and flowing, carrying us along in a stream of eloquence. The words are formal and dignified.

Pondering Lincoln's statements can move us to a proper stance of gratitude for national blessings. Additionally, the annual Thanksgiving that has been celebrated in the United States every November since Lincoln's proclamation is a source of tremendous spiritual and social blessing in the lives of Christians, so we may be appropriately thankful to God for this holiday itself. ▪

The Bible describes times when leaders summoned their people to express godly gratitude, as Abraham Lincoln did in the proclamation above. One of the greatest of these occasions was the dedication of the temple in Jerusalem. On that day, Solomon began his prayer with a grateful recollection of national blessing:

> Then Solomon stood before the altar of the LORD in the presence of all the assembly of Israel and spread out his hands toward heaven, and said, "O LORD, God of Israel, there is no God like you. . . . You have kept with your servant David my father what you declared to him." (1 Kings 8:22–23, 24)

We Thank You, O God

WILLIAM PATON MACKAY (1839–1885)

We thank you, O God,
For the Son of your love,
For Jesus who died
And is now gone above.

We thank you, O God,
For your Spirit of light,
Who has shown us our Savior
And scattered our night.

All glory and thanks
To the Lamb that was slain,
Who has borne all our sins
And has cleansed every stain.

All glory and thanks
To the God of all grace,
Who has bought us and sought us
And guided our ways.

Revive us again;
Fill each heart with your love;
May each soul be rekindled
With fire from above. ▪

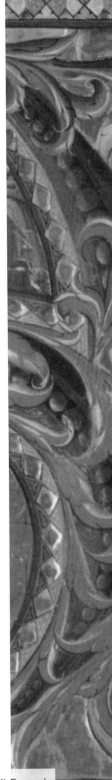

Lorenzo Monaco and Matteo di Filippo Torelli, Framed
Historiated "S" with Pentecost and Virgin Mary, early 1400s

THIS HYMNIC POEM IS A CORPORATE EXPRESSION of thanksgiving to God. Even though it is phrased in the plural, it is easy to read it as a personal statement as well. The defining characteristic of a thanksgiving poem or hymn is that it lists the blessings for which the speaker is grateful and then expresses thanks for those blessings. Whereas most thanksgiving poems and hymns take a wide-angle view, listing blessings in as many different areas as possible, this one takes the opposite approach. Its focus is single-mindedly on the work of redemption God has done in our lives. Although the original text of this hymn uses the word *praise*, its catalog of personally received blessings makes it more accurate to read it with the vocabulary of *thanks*.

One of the first things we notice about the poem is its winsome simplicity. Its lines are short and its rhyme scheme simple (*abcb*). The first two stanzas begin with the same opening line, and the third and fourth stanzas also begin with an identical first line of their own. Another thing that makes the poem easy to grasp is the way in which, from start to finish, it is a prayer addressed to God.

Until we get to its last stanza, the structure of the poem is likewise simple. The first two lines of each of its first four stanzas express thanks to God. Then the second pair of lines names the spiritual acts for which God is being thanked. It is clear that the poet is following a Trinitarian principle through his references to God the Father, the Son, and the Holy Spirit. More specifically, he is leading us to thank God the Father for sending his Son and his Spirit and for seeking and guiding us. We express gratitude to the Son for dying and for cleansing us from sin and to the Spirit for illuminating for us the truth about our Savior. This is a song of thanksgiving for our spiritual transformation from the lost state.

The simplicity of the poem comes to a sudden halt with the final stanza. Although standard editorial practice would allow us simply to omit a stanza from the original composition to produce a unified text, we gain something if we wrestle with the effect of a stanza of prayer about revival. What is the logic of such a prayer? One answer is that, as we contemplate the facets of our salvation for which the first four stanzas have led us to feel grateful, it is natural for us to long for an intensifying of our experience of salvation and of our gratitude for it.

The energetic meter of the poem plays a major role in its exuberant effect. All the poem's stanzas begin with an unaccented syllable that is followed by a pounding accented one: *we THANK*, *all GLORy*, and *reVIVE*.

After this pounding of the drum to capture our attention, everything that follows comes at the galloping pace of a meter known as anapestic—two unaccented syllables followed by an accented one: *for the SON of your LOVE*. Anapestic meter is a call for us to rouse ourselves and get moving.

The application is for us to allow the poem to express our own spirit of gratitude for salvation, along with our own prayer that it will revive our spiritual walk. ■

This hymn's focus on the supreme blessing of salvation is exactly the type of thanksgiving that the New Testament epistles also express. First Peter 1:3 captures the same spirit and sentiments: "Blessed be the God and Father of our Lord Jesus Christ! According to his great mercy, he has caused us to be born again to a living hope through the resurrection of Jesus Christ from the dead."

Master of Morgan 85, *Pentecost with Virgin Mary*, ca. 1515

Thanksgiving Song

KING DAVID

Oh give thanks to the Lord; call upon his name;
   make known his deeds among the peoples!
Sing to him, sing praises to him;
   tell of all his wondrous works!
Glory in his holy name;
   let the hearts of those who seek the Lord rejoice!
Seek the Lord and his strength;
   seek his presence continually!

Remember the wondrous works that he has done,
   his miracles and the judgments he uttered,
O offspring of Israel his servant,
   children of Jacob, his chosen ones!
He is the Lord our God;
   his judgments are in all the earth.

Remember his covenant forever,
   the word that he commanded, for a thousand generations,
the covenant that he made with Abraham,
   his sworn promise to Isaac,
which he confirmed to Jacob as a statute,
   to Israel as an everlasting covenant,
saying, "To you I will give the land of Canaan,
   as your portion for an inheritance."

When you were few in number,
   of little account, and sojourners in it,
wandering from nation to nation,
   from one kingdom to another people,
he allowed no one to oppress them;
   he rebuked kings on their account,
saying, "Touch not my anointed ones,
   do my prophets no harm!"

Sing to the Lord, all the earth!
   Tell of his salvation from day to day.
Declare his glory among the nations,
   his marvelous works among all the peoples!
For great is the Lord, and greatly to be praised,
   and he is to be feared above all gods.
For all the gods of the peoples are worthless idols,
   but the Lord made the heavens.
Splendor and majesty are before him;
   strength and joy are in his place.

Ascribe to the Lord, O families of the peoples,
   ascribe to the Lord glory and strength!
Ascribe to the Lord the glory due his name;
   bring an offering and come before him!
Worship the Lord in the splendor of holiness;
   tremble before him, all the earth;
   yes, the world is established; it shall never be moved.

Let the heavens be glad, and let the earth rejoice,
   and let them say among the nations, "The Lord reigns!"
Let the sea roar, and all that fills it;
   let the field exult, and everything in it!
Then shall the trees of the forest sing for joy
   before the Lord, for he comes to judge the earth.
Oh give thanks to the Lord, for he is good;
   for his steadfast love endures forever! ▪

THE FIRST CLUE THAT THIS POEM, recorded in 1 Chronicles 16:8–34, is a thanksgiving text is the fact that it is an *occasional poem*, meaning that it arose from a specific occasion. It is not a generalized, freestanding poem of praise. Instead it records David's grateful response to a blessed event that had just occurred.

The nature of the event is recorded in the seven verses that immediately precede the song. After the ark of God had been captured by the Philistines and recovered by the Israelites, David brought it to Jerusalem to reside in a tent he had prepared. This triumphant occasion took on qualities that may remind us of an American Thanksgiving. We read that David "distributed to all Israel, both men and women, to each a loaf of bread, a portion of meat, and a cake of raisins" (1 Chron. 16:3). That same day, David also appointed musicians to oversee worship at the site of the tent that housed the ark. "Then on that day David first appointed that thanksgiving be sung to the Lord" (v. 7).

Most poems have an *envelope structure*, meaning they signal their unifying element in their opening and closing lines. This song confirms that it is a thanksgiving song by beginning and ending with commands to *give thanks to the Lord*. Additionally, its second and third stanzas begin with commands to *remember*, which is a regular component of thanksgiving texts.

After three stanzas that command us to thank God and remember his acts, the poem's fourth stanza briefly gives us a reason for these commands: God's protection of Israel when it was a vulnerable, wandering nation. In stanzas 5 and 6, the song becomes more wide-ranging—it commands us to *sing, declare, ascribe glory, worship*, and *tremble*. This excursion into the motifs of praise and worship psalms has the effect of showing us how thanks interrelates with other religious postures. The final stanza returns to thanks and places its concluding command to *give thanks to the Lord* into a context of grand celebration, like that of a victory parade.

Having absorbed this song in terms of what it *meant* in its original context, we need to build bridges from it to our time and place and consider what it *means* now. For starters, the early chapters of covenant history, to which this poem refers, are our own history, inasmuch as all believers are the true Israel of God. Additionally, it is a truism that although literary texts are filled with particularized details, these particulars are a net by which such texts capture the universal. The feelings of thankfulness and celebration expressed in David's song are ones that we too feel, even though our experiences of them are different from David's.

The takeaway from this thanksgiving song resides in its combination of the technique of *apostrophe* (direct address, in this case to us as readers) with a continuous string of commands. If we follow these commands that are directly addressed to us, we will find ourselves participating in true thanksgiving. ■

This song of David is followed by a brief coda that encapsulates it: "Save us, O God of our salvation, and gather and deliver us from among the nations, that we may give thanks to your holy name and glory in your praise" (1 Chron. 16:35).

Johann Baptist Wenzel Bergl, Fresco in
Maria Dreieichen Basilica, 1771

Thankfulness Neglected

CHARLES SPURGEON (1834–1892)

OUR SUBJECT IS thankfulness to the Lord Jesus Christ.
. . . If you search the world around, among all choice
spices you shall scarcely meet with the frankincense of
gratitude. It ought to be as common as the dewdrops
that hang upon the hedges in the morning; but, alas, the
world is dry of thankfulness to God. . . .

There are more who receive benefits than ever give
praise for them. Nine persons healed, one person glorify-
ing God; nine persons healed of leprosy, mark you, and
only one person kneeling down at Jesus' feet, and thanking him for it. If for this surpassing benefit, which might
have made the dumb to sing, men only thank the Lord
in the proportion of one in ten, what shall I say of what
we call God's common mercies—only common because
he is so liberal with them, for each of them is inestima-
bly valuable? Life, health, eyesight, hearing, domestic
love, the continuance of friendships—I cannot attempt
a catalog of benefits that we receive every day; and yet is
there one man in ten that praises God for these? . . . We
receive a continent of mercies, and only return an island
of praise. . . . Sad it is to see God all goodness, and man all
ingratitude. . . .

Multitudes of our fellow citizens pray when they are
sick and near to dying, but when they grow better, their
praises grow sick unto death. The angel of mercy, listen-
ing at their door, has heard no canticle of love, no song of
thankfulness. . . . Should we get for ourselves so often a
drink from the rock of blessing, and so seldom pour out
a drink offering unto the Lord Most High? Come, let us
chide ourselves as we acknowledge that we offer so much
more prayer than praise. . . .

Let us consider the blessedness of thankfulness. This man was more blessed by far than the nine. They were healed, but they were not blessed as he was. There is a great blessedness in thankfulness. First, because it is right. Should not Christ be praised? This man did what he could, and there is always an ease of conscience, and a rest of Spirit, when you feel that you are doing all you can in a right cause. . . .

The next blessedness about praise is that it is acceptable to Christ. The Lord Jesus was evidently pleased; he was grieved to think the other nine did not come back, but he was charmed with this one man that he did return. . . . Whatever pleases Christ should be carefully cultivated by us. . . .

Let us learn from all this to put praise in a high place. . . . Let us think it as great a sin to neglect thanks as to restrain prayer. . . . Personal thanks to a personal Savior must be our life's objective. ■

The Bible passage on which Spurgeon builds his sermon is Luke 17:15–17:

> Then one of [the ten lepers], when he saw that he was healed, turned back . . . and fell on his face at Jesus' feet, giving him thanks. . . . Then Jesus answered, "Were not ten cleansed? Where are the nine?"

To catch the full import of this text, we need to transport our imaginations to London in 1886. We are seated with five thousand other people in a famous church called the Metropolitan Tabernacle. The preacher is the golden-tongued Charles Spurgeon. Everyone hangs on his words as he reads the account of Jesus' healing of ten lepers recorded in Luke 17:11–19. That story hinges on the contrast between the one leper who returned to thank Jesus and the remaining nine who did not.

Nearly every proverb in the Old Testament book of Proverbs either explicitly or implicitly commands a virtue while denouncing an opposing vice. This excerpt from Spurgeon's sermon adheres to this rhetoric of *antithesis* as, to move us to a life of gratitude, Spurgeon devotes half of his attention to the sin of *in*gratitude. Another name by which this technique is known is *foil*—meaning a contrast that *sets off* or heightens a subject. In this case, pondering ingratitude leads us to a fuller understanding of the sermon's announced subject: thankfulness to God.

Other techniques used here are borrowed from the prominent New Testament genre known as the *diatribe*, in which an audience is vigorously rebuked for its misconduct. This form of teaching and street preaching was common in the Greco-Roman world and appears in nearly all the epistles. In a diatribe, the author's energy is channeled into direct, "in your face" addresses to readers or listeners, an accusatory tone, the posing of rhetorical questions—not to elicit information but to express strong feeling—and the use of *aphorisms* (striking and memorable statements). Spurgeon's second and third paragraphs are textbook examples of these techniques. In these paragraphs, Spurgeon does not primarily offer an anatomy of ingratitude but instead chides us for it. The effect of this is to shame us for our negligence in expressing gratitude to God.

Then, with the transition *let us consider the blessedness of thankfulness*, we enter the realm of positive reinforcement. Having shown us the horrifying face of ingratitude, Spurgeon offers us something too wonderful to resist. After accomplishing this persuasive feat, he invites us in the final paragraph to make a switch from ingratitude to a life of thankfulness.

This excerpt's takeaway is twofold. Spurgeon rightly portrays ingratitude as a sin of omission—one that is usually begotten of lethargy and thoughtlessness. He invites us to repudiate such laziness and self-centeredness and, by contrast, to choose lives of thankfulness. ∎

Andrea Schiavone, *Christ Standing at the Right Healing the Lepers before Him*, ca. 1545

We Plow the Fields and Scatter

Mathias Claudius (1740–1815)

We plow the fields, and scatter
The good seed on the land,
But it is fed and watered
By God's almighty hand;
He sends the snow in winter,
The warmth to swell the grain,
The breezes and the sunshine,
And soft refreshing rain.

He only is the Maker
Of all things near and far;
He paints the wayside flower,
He lights the evening star;
The winds and waves obey him,
By him the birds are fed;
Much more to us, his children,
He gives our daily bread.

We thank thee, then, O Father,
For all things bright and good,
The seed time and the harvest,
Our life, our health, our food:
No gifts have we to offer
For all thy love imparts,
But that which thou desirest,
Our humble, thankful hearts.

Refrain
All good gifts around us
Are sent from heaven above,
Then thank the Lord, O thank the Lord
For all his love. ■

This text began as a seventeen-stanza German poem composed by Mathias Claudius and built around the motif of peasants gathering for a banquet and singing a song. Then a British translator of German hymns chose six of its stanzas to teach to children at an Anglican parish school in London, after which his text became an iconic harvest hymn in England. Through its usage there, this poem further evolved to become one of the five most familiar thanksgiving hymns sung at traditional church services in the United States.

When we turn to the text itself, we see that its first two stanzas do not, by themselves, signal the theme of thanksgiving. They are instead a nature poem in miniature. The focus of the first stanza is agricultural (doubtless influenced by the fact that the original author spent a stint as commissioner of agriculture in a region in Germany), while the second stanza broadens the scope to encompass nature more generally. Although these two stanzas do not use the vocabulary of thanks, we can easily slant them in that direction. The theme of God's provision in nature and elsewhere naturally prepares us to give thanks to him.

Johann Christian Klengel,
Harvest Landscape, 1809

But we are not left to our own designs to make that move, because the opening line of the third stanza does it for us. In view of God's provision for us through the forces of nature, *We thank thee, then, O Father.* The word *then,* which means *therefore,* has the force of a logical argument. As a consequence of the first two stanzas' rehearsal of God's providential acts, we naturally and logically thank him for them. This point is reinforced by the concluding lines of stanza 3, which declare that what God desires in return for the blessings he has bestowed on us is *our humble, thankful hearts.*

The refrain likewise anchors this hymn in the theme of thanksgiving. Its first two lines reiterate the providential theme that *all good gifts* in our lives *are sent from heaven above.* We should *then* (or *therefore*) *thank the Lord.* Even though the beginning of the hymn is somewhat remote from the theme of thanksgiving, its total package hangs together as a thanksgiving hymn, not a nature poem or a harvest poem.

As we absorb this hymnic poem in the manner we have just outlined, we can resolve to be more consciously aware that *all good gifts around us are sent from heaven above* and that God therefore merits our thanks for them. ■

This poem echoes numerous psalms that list God's acts of provision through nature as a picture of the care he shows people and as a reason for gratitude. Psalm 104 is the grandest example of these—here is an excerpt (vv. 13–14):

From your lofty abode you water the mountains;
    the earth is satisfied with the fruit of your work.

You cause the grass to grow for the livestock
    and plants for man to cultivate,
that he may bring forth food from the earth.

Model of a Man Plowing
(Egypt), ca. 1981–1885 BC

Thanksgiving Prayer

AUTHOR UNKNOWN

For flowers that bloom about our feet,
For tender grass, so fresh, so sweet,
For song of bird, and hum of bee,
For all things fair we hear or see,
  Father in heaven, we thank you.

For blue of stream and blue of sky,
For pleasant shade of branches high,
For fragrant air and cooling breeze,
For beauty of the blooming trees,
  Father in heaven, we thank you.

For mother love and father care,
For brothers strong and sisters fair,
For love at home and here each day,
For guidance lest we go astray,
  Father in heaven, we thank you.

For this new morning with its light,
For rest and shelter of the night,
For health and food, for love and friends,
For everything your goodness sends,
  Father in heaven, we thank you.

Martin Johnson Heade, *Cattleya Orchid
and Three Hummingbirds*, 1871

THIS POEM EXPRESSES THANKS TO God for what the Puritans quaintly called "the creatures"—meaning the earthly pleasures that we experience as part of God's created order. One Puritan sounded the keynote of this concept when he wrote, paraphrasing 1 Timothy 4:4, that "the creatures of God are to be received with thanksgiving." Another framework that can help us to understand the argument of the poem is a distinction that earlier eras made between the order of nature and the order of grace. The order of nature encompassed human life, in the physical and earthly sphere, along with the knowledge we derive from the light of reason. The order of grace encompassed the spiritual and supernatural realm as well as the knowledge derived from the Bible's divine revelation. No work of literature can cover all that could be said on a subject, and it is no mark against this thanksgiving prayer that it limits its focus to the blessings of human life in this world.

Before looking in more detail at the content of this poem, we should note its format. Every line, except the refrain line at the end of each stanza,

The Tree of Life (British),
early to mid 1600s

begins with the preposition *for* and then follows it by naming one or more blessings. The poem as a whole thus adheres to the catalog structure of the thanksgiving poem genre. Ordinarily this degree of repetition would create monotony, but in this case it does not. The poem's *syntax*, or sentence structure, grabs our attention—and does so through two techniques. The first is *inversion*—whereas ordinarily the subject of a sentence comes first and the predicate (that which describes the action) comes second, here they come in the opposite order. Adding to an effect of the extraordinary is the fact that each stanza forms a *suspended sentence*—one that we need to keep reading until finally, at the very end, its line of thinking is completed. This technique produces growing tension and suspense, which in turn heightens our attention.

The refrain line packs a big punch in multiple ways. It finally completes each stanza's suspended sentence, allowing us to relax. It also causes the order of nature, which has dominated the first four lines of each stanza, to give way to the greater order of grace as it also moves from the blessings of earthly life to the divine giver of those blessings. In keeping with the poem's providential theme, the refrain specifically invokes God's role as father. Finally, it transforms the poem's list of blessings into the prayer that its title has declared it to be in advance.

Looking more minutely at the catalog of blessings, we should note that its first two stanzas are a nature poem, which evokes our own favorite images of nature, and which is balanced and complemented by the domestic focus of the third stanza and climaxed by the wide-angle scope of the last stanza.

This is an archetypal "feel good" poem, and we should free ourselves to experience it as such. We can return to it as a never-failing source of uplift for the day. ■

First Timothy 4:4 provides a doctrinal foundation for the movement of thought that this poem expresses: "Everything created by God is good, and nothing is to be rejected if it is received with thanksgiving."

Bee-shaped ornament
(Korea), ca. 918–1392

Why Our Prayers Must Include Thanksgiving

John Calvin (1509–1564)

In our requests and petitions, we pour out our desires before God, imploring those things that tend to the propagation of his glory . . . and to our own advantage. In thanksgiving, we celebrate his goodness toward us with due praises, acknowledging all the blessings we have received as the gifts of his liberality. Therefore David has connected these two parts together: "Call upon me in the day of trouble; I will deliver you, and you shall glorify me" (Ps. 50:15). Scripture commands the continual use of both petition and thanksgiving.

Our needs are so great, . . . and we are oppressed on every side with such numerous and great perplexities, that we all have sufficient cause for ardent supplications to God. . . . But in the sacrifice of praise and thanksgiving . . . we are inactive and sluggish. . . . Our sacrifice of praise and thanksgiving should be continual, since God ceases not to accumulate on us his various benefits . . . in order to constrain us . . . to the exercise of gratitude. Furthermore, we are almost overwhelmed with such great and copious effusions of his beneficence, and we are surrounded wherever we turn our eyes by such numerous and amazing miracles of his hand, that we never lack substance for praise and thanksgiving. . . .

Since God is justly honored when he is acknowledged to be the Author of all blessings, it follows that they should all be so received from his hand as to be attended with unceasing thanksgiving, and that there is no other proper method of using the benefits that flow to us from his goodness except by continual acknowledgments of his praise, and unceasing expressions of our gratitude. . . . Wherefore David, after experiencing the goodness of the Lord, beautifully declares, "He has put a new song in my mouth" (Ps. 40:3), whereby he certainly implies that we are guilty of a criminal silence if we omit to praise him for any benefit, since in every blessing he bestows on us he gives us additional cause to bless his name. . . .

Whenever believers entreat the Lord to do anything *for his name's sake*, . . . they place themselves under an obligation to thanksgiving, and promise that the divine beneficence shall be productive of this proper effect on them, even to cause them to celebrate its fame. . . . Nor do the divine blessings claim only the praises of the tongue, but naturally call forth our love. . . . Nor will any praises ever please God except such as flow from this ardor of love. . . .

God lays us under a sacred obligation to sing his praises whenever he grants us the enjoyment of our wishes. . . . This is the reason Paul directs to "pray without ceasing" and "in everything to give thanks" (1 Thess. 5:17–18), because he desires that all people, with all possible persistence, at every time and in every place, and in all circumstances and affairs, may direct their prayers to God, expecting all from him, and ascribing to him the praise of all, since he affords us perpetual matter of prayer and thanksgiving. ■

ONE ADVANTAGE OF AN ANTHOLOGY is that it may show how many-faceted its subject is. As its succession of entries turns the prism in the light, certain entries fill a specific niche in our understanding. When it comes to the topic of thanksgiving, this passage, by John Calvin, is one such entry. Calvin addresses a problem that is common to our prayer lives, namely, the overwhelming preponderance of petitions in our daily prayers.

We should pause to note the unexpected place where Calvin's excursion into the subject of prayer occurs. Today we might expect such words,

Léon Henri Antoine Loire, *Man, Woman, and Girl at Prayer in Church*, 1864 exhorting and encouraging us to pursue excellence in prayer, to appear in a pastor's internet blog or congregational newsletter. Yet the source of these is actually one of the most famous treatises of foundational Christian theology ever written: *Institutes of the Christian Religion.* Although we ordinarily expect a theological treatise to inform our minds, this passage has a persuasive cast because the author hopes to move us to remedy a problem in our spiritual walk.

As we might expect from a theologian, Calvin takes an analytic approach to his subject. The logical argument of the passage unfolds as follows: First it leads us to ponder why our prayers are weighted so heavily in the direction of petition. Then it gives us the reason that *our needs are so great* that it is natural for us to pour out *ardent supplications to God.* Although the general tenor of Calvin's remarks is one of criticism, he begins from a stance of compassionate understanding.

Having briefly conceded that our problem is understandable, Calvin next analyzes at length why our tendency to overweight our prayers with petitions is unacceptable. Chief among the reasons is the sheer abundance of the blessings God has bestowed on us, so that *we never lack substance for . . . thanksgiving.* In fact, *we are guilty of a criminal silence* if we do not thank *the Author of all blessings* for his beneficence.

After chastising us for being *inactive and sluggish* about thanking God, Calvin offers reasons, and implied incentives, for us to thank God in the same proportion at which we petition him to meet our needs. Among his arguments are that (1) when we thank God, he is *justly honored* as the giver of all that we receive, (2) *Scripture commands the continual use of both petition and thanksgiving,* and (3) *God lays us under a sacred obligation to sing his praises whenever he grants us . . . our wishes.*

We should accept Calvin's admonitions and persuasions as a welcome solution to a problem that burdens us. Calvin, in effect, gives us a spiritual pep talk to be all that we can be—and all that God wants us to be—in our prayer lives. ▪

Calvin's opening paragraph sets forth the proposition that our prayers must combine petition and thanksgiving. The classic New Testament statement of this principle is Philippians 4:6: "In everything by prayer and supplication with thanksgiving let your requests be made known to God."

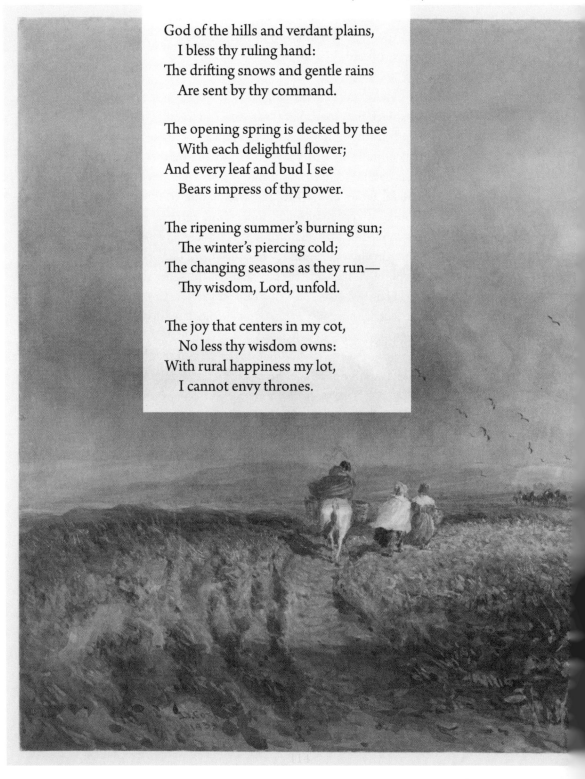

Hymn of Gratitude

Daniel C. Colesworthy (1810–1893)

God of the hills and verdant plains,
  I bless thy ruling hand:
The drifting snows and gentle rains
  Are sent by thy command.

The opening spring is decked by thee
  With each delightful flower;
And every leaf and bud I see
  Bears impress of thy power.

The ripening summer's burning sun;
  The winter's piercing cold;
The changing seasons as they run—
  Thy wisdom, Lord, unfold.

The joy that centers in my cot,
  No less thy wisdom owns:
With rural happiness my lot,
  I cannot envy thrones.

Love dwells within my peaceful breast
  At every morning's dawn;
And when the sun sinks in the west,
  My cares are all withdrawn.

Beside the hill, the purling brook,
  Glad Nature's fond retreat,
With gratitude to Thee I look,
  And songs of joy repeat.

For lot so blest, my voice I raise,
  Almighty God, to thee!
Thou needest not an angel's praise;
  Much less such praise from me.

But I will bless thy bounteous hand
  For all the gifts bestowed:
Before my heart could understand,
  Ten thousand thanks I owed. ◼

GRATITUDE IS NOT A SELF-CONTAINED VIRTUE. Instead, it is nurtured by other virtues, such as humility and contentment. It has been said that a proud person is seldom a grateful person. "Hymn of Gratitude" gives us the inverse of that dictum by voicing the gratitude of a humble soul.

The poet was a prolific nineteenth-century New England author and printer of material for the young. On the surface, his hymn is an expression of the Quaker enjoyment of simple pleasures and embrace of the unaspiring life. It catalogs the pleasant features of life as experienced by those who endorse such ideals. As we look closely at the unfolding list that the poem presents, we can see the plan behind its organization take shape. In the first three stanzas, the poet lingers briefly but lovingly on the seasonal cycles of nature that he has known in his native Maine and during his adult life in Boston.

Then, in the next three stanzas, the poet becomes introspective and analytic. He ponders the joy that he has described in the first three stanzas. Perhaps he is recording a moment of discovery, perhaps sharing a long-held philosophy. In either case, he chooses contentment—and not an amorphous contentment but one that is linked to nature and rural living.

This poem aligns itself—particularly in its middle three stanzas—with a very ancient literary tradition known as the *pastoral tradition*. There is a metaphoric or symbolic principle at work here. It is not that the speaker thinks we need to live in the country in order to live a happy and contented life of gratitude. Rather, he asks us to embrace the spirit and emotions that his images of a humble rural life invoke.

The poem's last two stanzas move from celebrating a contented life to making a statement of resolution, as the speaker commits himself to living a life of gratitude. The note of gratitude that has been latent throughout his praising of simple pleasures now becomes a manifesto. It does not simply celebrate the pleasures of a certain kind of life; it is, even more importantly, a prayer addressed to God. Its opening line is an invocation, and from then on it intermittently reminds us that its speaker is addressing God in prayer.

The last stanza invites us to join the poet in his resolution to live a life of gratitude to God for his *bounteous hand*. The takeaway is for us to accept the poem's invitation. ▪

previous: David Cox,
Journey Home, 1833

Colesworthy's prayer of humility before God reminds us of another poet's stance: "Lord, my heart is not haughty, nor mine eyes lofty: neither do I exercise myself in great matters, or in things too high for me" (Ps. 131:1 KJV). While not itself an expression of gratitude, such humility is a promising seedbed from which gratitude can grow.

New England Farm in Winter, 1850 or after

Blest Be the Tie That Binds

JOHN FAWCETT (1739–1817)

Blest be the tie that binds
Our hearts in Christian love;
The fellowship of kindred minds
Is like to that above.

Before our Father's throne
We pour our ardent prayers;
Our fears, our hopes, our aims are one,
Our comforts and our cares.

We share each other's woes,
Our mutual burdens bear;
And often for each other flows
The sympathizing tear.

When we asunder part,
It gives us inward pain;
But we shall still be joined in heart,
And hope to meet again.

This glorious hope revives
Our courage by the way;
While each in expectation lives,
And longs to see the day.

From sorrow, toil and pain,
And sin, we shall be free,
And perfect love and friendship reign
Through all eternity. ■

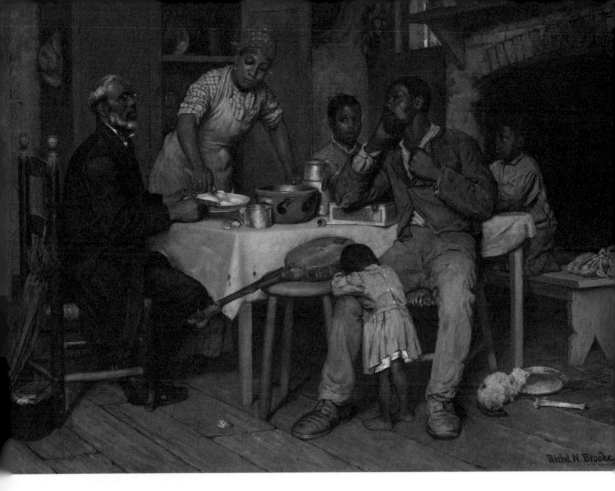

THE POEM "BLEST BE THE TIE THAT BINDS" has become a standard hymn to sing at communion services and farewells. But is it a thanksgiving hymn as well? It is—and the first tip-off is the story of its origin.

Its author, John Fawcett, was a dissenting Baptist minister in an impoverished farming community in Yorkshire, England. He could have become one of the most prominent preachers and scholars in the country, and his first opportunity in that direction came when he accepted a call to pastor the prestigious Carter's Lane Baptist Church in London. Preparing for the move, he and his wife, Mary, disbursed their larger furniture and many of Fawcett's books. He even preached his farewell sermon.

The day of their departure came. Their goods were loaded onto a cart as the parishioners looked on, weeping. First Mary and then Fawcett himself were so overcome with emotion that they decided on the spot to stay. On the Sunday after this emotional decision, Fawcett preached on Luke 12:15: "A man's life consisteth not in the abundance of the things which he possesseth" (KJV). He closed his sermon by reading a poem he had composed and titled "Brotherly Love." This eventually became the hymn

Richard Norris Brooke,
A Pastoral Visit, 1881

"Blest Be the Tie That Binds." What was the author's emotional state as he composed this poem? He felt an overwhelming sense of gratitude for the people of his church and for the spiritual bond that he and his wife shared with them.

The topic of this hymnic poem is not simply Christian fellowship (the feelings Christians share when they are physically together) but the spiritual bond that joins them even when they are not physically present with one another. Stanza by stanza, the poem lists the specific blessings that this bond confers. The resulting genre is the *charter*—a declaration of the privileges that people possess by virtue of their membership in a group.

The poem's unifying theme is thus the blessedness of the spiritual union that believers share with one another in Christ. The variations in each stanza are as follows: (1) mutual love and kindred minds, which are akin to what exists in heaven; (2) a wide-ranging (but mainly positive) catalog of shared life experiences; (3) the sharing of life's difficult experiences; (4) mutual pain and consolation in the event of physical parting; (5) a celebration of how the hope of heavenly reunion sustains separated believers; (6) a vision of heavenly perfection and eternal union. Each stanza leads naturally and logically to the next in a seamless pattern.

This poem does not exist to impart information about the blessedness of the unity that believers share in Christ. Instead it celebrates that bond and awakens our gratitude for it. We ourselves can take the further step of expressing thanks to God for what the poem celebrates. ■

Ephesians 4:4–6 makes the same declaration as Fawcett's poem.

> There is one body and one Spirit—just as you were called to the one hope that belongs to your call—one Lord, one faith, one baptism, one God and father of all, who is over all and through all and in all.

A formula found in other New Testament epistles springs naturally to mind as well: "Thanks be to God."

Winslow Homer,
Cannon Rock, 1895

How Gratitude Transformed a Life

DANIEL DEFOE (1660–1731), *ROBINSON CRUSOE*

WHILE I WAS thus gathering strength, my thoughts ran exceedingly upon the Scripture passage, "I will deliver thee." The impossibility of my deliverance [from the island on which I was a castaway] lay much upon my mind. . . . Then it occurred to my mind that I pored so much upon my deliverance from the main affliction [of being a solitary castaway] that I disregarded the deliverance I had already received, and I was made to ask myself such questions as these: Have I not been delivered from sickness—from the most distressed condition that could be . . . ? And what notice had I taken of it? Had I done my part? God had delivered me, but I had not glorified Him—that is to say, I had not owned and been thankful for that as a deliverance. And how could I expect greater deliverance? This touched my heart very much, and immediately I knelt down and gave God thanks aloud for my recovery from my sickness.

In the morning I took the Bible, and beginning at the New Testament, I began seriously to read it. . . . It was not long after . . . that I found my heart more deeply and sincerely affected with the wickedness of my past life. . . . It happened providentially that the very day of reading the Scripture, I came to these words: "He is exalted a Prince and a Savior, to give repentance and to give remission." I threw down the book, and with my heart as well as my hands lifted up to heaven, in a kind of ecstasy of joy, I cried out aloud, "Jesus, thou son of David! Jesus, thou exalted Prince and Savior! give me repentance!" This was the first time I could say, in the true sense of the words, that I prayed in all my life, for now I prayed with a sense of my condition, and a true Scripture view of hope, founded on the encouragement of the Word of God. . . .

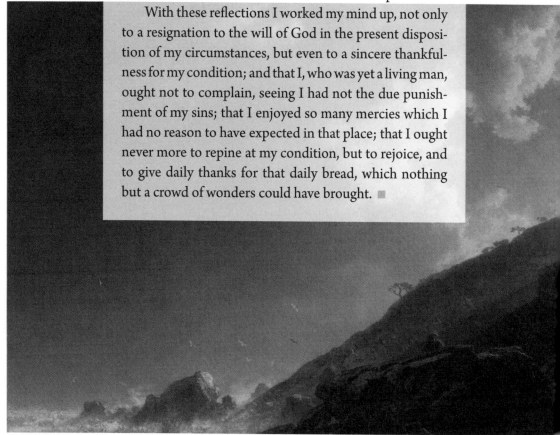

From this moment I began to conclude in my mind that it was possible for me to be happy in this forsaken, solitary condition . . . , and with this thought I was going to give thanks to God. . . . I sincerely gave thanks to God for opening my eyes, by whatever afflicting providences, to see the former condition of my life, and to mourn for my wickedness, and repent. I never opened the Bible, or shut it, but my very soul within me blessed God for directing my friend in England, without any order of mine, to pack [my Bible] among my goods, and for assisting me afterwards to save it out of the wreck of the ship. . . .

With these reflections I worked my mind up, not only to a resignation to the will of God in the present disposition of my circumstances, but even to a sincere thankfulness for my condition; and that I, who was yet a living man, ought not to complain, seeing I had not the due punishment of my sins; that I enjoyed so many mercies which I had no reason to have expected in that place; that I ought never more to repine at my condition, but to rejoice, and to give daily thanks for that daily bread, which nothing but a crowd of wonders could have brought. ∎

DANIEL DEFOE IS A MAJOR figure in English literature. He was also an ardent dissenter and Presbyterian who was intermittently persecuted and imprisoned for his religious convictions. As legacy of his commitment, he was buried in Bunhill Fields, a nonconformist cemetery in London, where a monument to him stands within sight of John Bunyan's sarcophagus.

The passage printed above recounts the turning point in the life of Defoe's fictional protagonist Robinson Crusoe. The novel that shares his name is the original and prototypical castaway story in English literature. It spawned many successors, including *The Swiss Family Robinson*. Defoe's story traces the adventures of a man who suffers shipwreck while running away from home in rejection of his father. It is mainly the story of his survival on a lonely island. In the excerpt printed above, he is convicted of his sinfulness and turns to God.

Andreas Achenbach, *Sunset after a Storm on the Coast of Sicily*, 1853

It is the specific way that Defoe chose to portray Crusoe's conversion that makes this passage a fitting inclusion in this anthology of thanksgiving writings. The sin for which Crusoe stands convicted is ingratitude to God for the deliverances he has experienced from many hardships and crises on the island. Crusoe's conversion expresses itself most fully in his resolve to live in thankfulness to God.

As we go on to analyze what this passage teaches us about gratitude, we need to remind ourselves of how fiction conveys truth. Biography, history, and the daily news tell us what *happened*, while fiction and literature tell us what *happens*. Literature is *truthful to human experience*, and the fact that it records an imagined person's experience rather than a real-life event detracts nothing from its ability to delineate the truth about life— in this case, the truth about gratitude.

The passage shows us three things about gratitude. First, Defoe does a masterful job of portraying the ignominy of ingratitude by taking us inside his protagonist's thought process at the very moment of his conviction of sin. Crusoe begins the passage by tallying up the times God has providentially delivered him and is shocked by his ingratitude after being rescued from so many threats. Second, Defoe leads us to see that thanksgiving is a necessary part of the redeemed life. Crusoe resolves not only *to be happy in [his] forsaken, solitary condition* but also *to give thanks to God*. Third, the final paragraph of the excerpt leads us to see that living a life of gratitude requires us to resolve to be thankful by showing us that Crusoe *worked [his] mind up* to *give daily thanks to God*.

The lessons and resolve that Defoe's fictional protagonist shares with the world are something we likewise can learn and put into practice. ▪

Robinson Crusoe learned to give thanks to God long after surviving a shipwreck. Acts 27 recounts how Paul similarly survived a shipwreck, but it records that the apostle gave thanks in the midst of the storm rather than long after it: "When he had said these things, he took bread, and giving thanks to God in the presence of all [the passengers on the ship] he broke it and began to eat" (v. 35). We can all give thanks as we endure our metaphoric storms and shipwrecks in life.

Jean Fouquet, *The Right Hand of God Protecting the Faithful against the Demons*, ca. 1452–1460

We Gather Together

ANONYMOUS (1597)

We gather together to ask the Lord's blessing;
He chastens and hastens his will to make known;
The wicked oppressing now cease from distressing:
Sing praise to his Name; he forgets not his own.

Beside us to guide us, our God with us joining,
Ordaining, maintaining his kingdom divine;
So from the beginning the fight we were winning:
Thou, Lord, were at our side: all glory be thine!

We all do extol thee, thou leader triumphant,
And pray that thou still our defender wilt be.
Let thy congregation escape tribulation:
Thy Name be ever praised! O Lord, make us free! ∎

Through the years, "We Gather Together" has been a fixture at American Thanksgiving services. It is a Thanksgiving hymn by usage, so when we sing it at a church service, we assimilate it as a hymn of thanks, no further questions asked. These preliminary comments are necessary because, when we look closely at the hymn's content, it does not obviously appear to be a thanksgiving text. Its opening line, for example, claims that we gather together not to thank the Lord but to ask his blessing. This does not mean that the poem is not a thanksgiving hymn—only that it requires unpacking to reveal its true nature.

The poem began its life in the Netherlands, in 1597, when it was composed to celebrate a military victory Dutch Protestants had won over Spanish Catholics. It is easy to imagine that a patriotic hymn celebrating a military rescue was sung in a spirit of gratitude. The original Puritan settlers of New England would have known this Dutch patriotic hymn by virtue of their residence in the Netherlands for a decade before they came to North America. The poem as we know it is a translation composed in 1894 by Theodore Baker, who called it "a prayer of thanksgiving."

As we take our cue from these considerations, the thanksgiving features of the poem begin to take shape. Although its content is varied, its primary element is a catalog of God's acts on behalf of his people, and such a catalog of blessings is the backbone of all thanksgiving poems. Although the acts of national deliverance that the poem describes originally referred to a military victory at a specific time and place, the poet phrases the situation in sufficiently universal terms for us to readily apply his assertions to our own nations, our own families, and our own individual lives. God is always *at our side*.

Additionally, we need to probe the poem's opening three words, *we gather together*, for Thanksgiving overtones. First, Thanksgiving is the preeminent holiday on which American families gather together. In our grocery stores come Thanksgiving season, we find napkins and paper plates with autumn images accompanied by the single word *Gather*. It is a code word for Thanksgiving. *Gather* also brings to mind the magical words from Edward Winslow's account of the first New England thanksgiving: *our harvest being gotten [gathered] in*. Aspects of harvest and the end of the growing season are part of the deep structure of the annual Thanksgiving, and the vocabulary of gathering is a part.

As we sing this hymn and ponder its turns of phrase, we can thank God for his specific acts of rescue and victory in our own lives. A military victory in 1597 can become a metaphor for what God has done for us throughout the year as we reflect on it at the end of November. ■

"We Gather Together" thanks God for delivering his people from the enemies and tribulations in their lives. Psalm 34:6–7 is a parallel passage.

> This poor man cried, and the LORD heard him
>> and saved him out of all his troubles.
> The angel of the LORD encamps
>> around those who fear him, and delivers them.

Worthington Whittredge,
The Camp Meeting, 1874

Reflections on Gratitude

You sanctify whatever you are grateful for. (Anthony De Mello)

On Thanksgiving Day we acknowledge our dependence. (William Jennings Bryan)

We are in a wrong state of mind if we are not in a thankful state of mind. (Charles Spurgeon)

We should spend as much time in thanking God for his benefits as we do in asking him for them. (Vincent de Paul)

The chief sacrifice that God requires at people's hands is that they should acknowledge his benefits and be thankful to him for them. (John Calvin)

When it comes to life, the critical thing is whether you take things for granted or take them with gratitude. (G. K. Chesterton).

THE KEY TO ASSIMILATING THIS compilation of "quotable quotes" is to be aware of something called *aphoristic thinking*, also known as *proverbial thinking*. An *aphorism* or *proverb* is a concise, memorable statement of truth. It is a self-contained sentence, not a paragraph with unifying topics and supporting data. From ancient times to the present day, many cultures and groups have attached great importance to proverbs. This is especially true of cultures and groups whose knowledge is stored and passed on orally.

Proverbs are a literary form that has its own traits and rules of operation. A good proverb not only *states* an insight but is often so striking that it *compels* or *triggers* an insight. A good proverb is often based on common knowledge, so that it seems familiar, but it will also add an original twist to received wisdom.

The magic of a proverb is that it is intended not to put an end to our thinking about a given topic but instead to be a starting point. This requires an active reader, so when we approach this collection of aphorisms about gratitude, we need to do our share: we must resist any thought of speed-reading and instead settle down to a slow and meditative process of reading and thinking.

Proverbs are able to achieve their effect because of their literary features. Conciseness is their chief trait, which they employ by stripping an area of life down to a core principle. They achieve memorability, as well, through verbal beauty and originality of thought. In addition, most proverbs are built on a principle of balance: their first half introduces a subject and their second half, after we take a mental pause, completes the thought.

The proverbs printed above will yield more and more insights as we ponder them. The following tips will start this process. Most writing about thanksgiving focuses on the benefits that will result, for both God and ourselves, from our being thankful; De Mello's proverb directs our attention instead to the *objects* for we are thankful, and it makes the

unexpected claim that these things themselves are sanctified by our gratitude for them. Americans are geared to celebrate their national independence on July 4; Bryan plays off this holiday motif with his claim that, on Thanksgiving, we acknowledge our *de*pendence. Spurgeon similarly gains his effect by evoking a common saying about being in the right state of mind, but he reverses it by speaking of being in a wrong state of mind. Vincent de Paul's dictum convicts us about our prayers' preponderance of petition over thanks, and Calvin challenges our common assumption that feats of action are what God desires from us. Finally, we most naturally assume that the opposite of gratitude is ingratitude, but Chesterton proposes instead that its actual opposite is taking blessings for granted.

Some of the best thinking about gratitude is enshrined in aphorisms. The collection of proverbs in this entry is an invitation for us to drink deeply at the fountain of truth about gratitude and then to find ways of applying these gems of truth to our real-life situations. ▪

The Bible enshrines much of its teaching about thanksgiving in aphorisms such as the following: "The one who offers thanksgiving as his sacrifice glorifies me" (Ps. 50:23).

previous: Albert Pinkham Ryder, *Harvest*, no date;
Mary Cassatt, *The Map*, 1890

Thanksgiving

Kate Louise Wheeler (dates unknown)

Not because you givest me
Life from care and sorrow free,
Do I thank you, Lord, today,
But because in life's dark hour
You have given peace and power
To sustain me on the way.

Not for gift of wealth or fame
Do I praise your kingly name,
Kneeling now with grateful heart,
But for home, for friends, and health—
Greater gifts than fame or wealth,
Blessings of my life a part.

Not because the earth is bright
With a wealth of joy and light
Do I thank you, Lord Divine,
But because in home above
Life eternal speaks your love,
And the hope of heaven is mine. ■

WRITTEN BY A LITTLE-KNOWN New Hampshire poet of the late nineteenth century, this poem is cast as a prayer. The effect is that we overhear a conversation in a confessional mode in which the speaker takes God into her confidence. As we listen, we get the impression that she is also correcting a misconception that has been circulating about her.

An obvious symmetry underlies the poem's stanzas. The skeleton of this symmetry is a rhetorical pattern of "not . . . but." In the first three lines of each stanza, the speaker outlines what her gratitude is *not* "because of" or "for." The word *but* at the beginning of each fourth line then initiates a contrast. Having dismissed what she is *not* thanking God for, the speaker states what *is* the cause of the thanksgiving she has named in the poem's title.

As we look more closely at the two halves of this pattern, we see a degree of subtlety to this seemingly simple poem. What the speaker dismisses as being of inferior value is what today we call the "success ethic"—a life free from tragedy and anxiety (stanza 1), a celebrity life of wealth and fame (stanza 2), and more generally a world dominated by joy and a symbolic light (stanza 3). All of this adds up to what the human race celebrates and aspires to have. Yet in the value system that this poem espouses, these things are of inferior worth—and, in fact, they are beyond our reach and therefore an illusion.

What, then, constitutes reality as understood in this poem? Two things. In its first and third stanzas, the blessings that the speaker describes being

grateful for are solidly spiritual in nature: the sustaining power of God during the dark experiences of life and the hope of an eternal home in heaven. The middle stanza's blessings are human rather than spiritual, yet they still share the other two stanzas' quality of being humble blessings that lack the ostentation of the rich and famous: the blessings of *home*, *friends*, and *health*.

This poem offers a corrective to the prevailing wish list of materialistic and success-oriented societies. The values that it espouses have both a spiritual aspect and a social one. Their spiritual aspect centers on God's sustaining presence and the prospect of eternal life in heaven. On their social level, the values that the poem embraces can be called homespun values. The poet binds these two aspects together in the last stanza, when she portrays heaven—a spiritual reality—using the domestic image of a home.

This poem of simple piety can serve as a reality check for us—a corrective against the allure of worldly-mindedness and a realignment toward the primacy of the spiritual. ▪

The corrective offered by this poem is based on the principle found in 2 Corinthians 4:18: "We look not to the things that are seen but to the things that are unseen. For the things that are seen are transient, but the things that are unseen are eternal."

George Inness, *Sundown*, 1884

Rendering Thanks to Our Maker

Martin Luther (1483–1546)

What do we mean when we affirm that we believe in God the Father Almighty, maker of heaven and earth? This is what I mean and believe: that I am a creature of God, that he has given and constantly preserves my body, soul, and life, all my senses, reason, and understanding, and so on, food and drink, clothing and support, wife and children, house and home. He also causes all creatures to serve for the uses and necessities of life—sun, moon and stars in the firmament, day and night, air, fire, water, earth, and whatever it bears and produces, birds and fishes, beasts, grain, and all kinds of produce, and whatever else there is of bodily and temporal goods, good government, peace, and security. . . .

God the Father has not only given us all that we have and see before our eyes, but daily preserves and defends us against evil and misfortune, and averts all sorts of danger and calamity. He does all this out of pure love and goodness, without our merit, as a benevolent Father, who cares for us that no evil befall us. . . . Therefore, since all that we possess . . . is daily given, preserved, and kept for us by God, it is obvious that it is our duty to love, praise, and thank him for it without ceasing, and to serve him with all these things as he demands and has enjoined.

How few there are who truly believe this article of the Apostles' Creed. For we all pass over it, hear it and say it, but neither see nor consider what the words teach us. For if we believed it with the heart, we would also act accordingly, and not . . . boast as though we had life, riches, power, and honor, etc., of ourselves, . . . and neglect to thank him or acknowledge him as Lord and Creator. . . .

We ought, therefore, daily to thank God as creator of all things, impress it upon our mind, and to remember it in all that meets our eyes, and in all good that falls to our lot, and wherever we escape from calamity or danger, that it is God who gives and does all these things, that therein we sense and see his paternal heart and his transcendent love toward us. Thereby the heart would be warmed and kindled to be thankful, and to employ all such good things to the honor and praise of God.

We see, then, what we have and receive from God, and what we owe in return. . . . But we have a far greater treasure . . . in that the Father has given himself to us, together with all creatures, and has most richly provided for us in this life, and in addition he has overwhelmed us with unspeakable, eternal treasures by his Son and Holy Spirit. ▪

THE PROSE ENTRIES IN THIS ANTHOLOGY are not examples of expository or informational prose, such as we find in essays and news magazines. These classic texts are devotional—in both technique and effect. Their literary form captivates us and remains in our memory. They do not carry all of their meaning on the surface; they require us to unpack them. This unpacking often turns upon a paradoxical or surprising or dissonant aspect of them that we need to resolve.

The passage by Martin Luther fits this pattern. Even before we look closely at its content, two surprises meet us. First, the passage appears in Luther's Large Catechism. We do not expect to find an extended meditation on thanksgiving in a catechism. Even more surprising is that Luther's entire discussion is based on a statement from the Apostles' Creed. This creed is a summary of Christian doctrine, not a springboard to a devotional. As we ponder these surprises, it becomes evident that Luther's aim is not to inform us. He has instead the devotional aim of orienting our minds and souls to behave in a certain way, namely, to live in thankfulness to God because he is the Creator. In keeping with this purpose, Luther does not share the *product* of his thinking on his subject but instead invites us to share his *process* of thinking this issue through.

The first stage of this thought process, as seen in paragraph 1, introduces his topic and defines it. In a manner similar to that of the prayer by John Donne that we saw earlier in this anthology, Luther takes us behind the scenes of our bodies, and the satisfaction of their daily needs, to show us how God superintends everything in the natural world to enable our survival. Then, in the second paragraph, he (1) builds on this insight with a summary statement about God's preservation of our lives, (2) asserts that this preservation demonstrates God's gracious benevolence to us, and (3) draws the logical conclusion that it is thus our duty to be thankful to our maker and preserver.

After laying all of these thoughts on the table, the passage next takes the introspective step of leading us to acknowledge our sinful neglect of proper gratitude. But the fourth paragraph, instead of leaving us paralyzed by guilt, quickly takes us by the hand and gives us an action plan for how we can live a life of gratitude to God for the gifts of life and providence he has given us. This plan is presented so winsomely that it would be perverse for us not to endorse it. The final paragraph serves as a textbook model of a closing statement, and even begins with exactly the right formula for one: *We see, then. . . .* And then, in the classic manner of a *peroration* or

climax, Luther adds a new idea that goes beyond what he has covered thus far: the Father of creation *has overwhelmed us* with *spiritual provisions by his Son and Holy Spirit.*

This entry from Luther's catechism is nothing short of a *primer* (a statement of first principles) on the implications of the doctrine that God is the maker of heaven and earth. The application we can take from it is to affirm Luther's line of thought in our own minds and to put his directives into practice. ▪

Luther's theme is the gratitude that we owe to God for his creation and providence. This is also the theme of selected verses in Psalm 145:

> The Lᴏʀᴅ is good to all,
>> and his mercy is over all that he has made.
>
> All your works shall give thanks to you, O Lᴏʀᴅ,
>> and all your saints shall bless you. (vv. 9–10)
>
> You open your hand;
>> you satisfy the desire of every living thing. (v. 16)

Pieter de Hooch, *The Bedroom,* 1658/1660

God's Gifts: Reasons to Be Thankful

There is nothing better for a person
    than that he should eat and drink
    and find enjoyment in his toil.
This also, I saw, is from the hand of God,
for apart from him who can eat
    or who can have enjoyment?

To the one who pleases him God has given
    wisdom and knowledge and joy.

I perceived that there is nothing better for them
    than to be joyful
    and to do good as long as they live;
also that everyone should eat and drink
    and take pleasure in all his toil—
    this is God's gift to man.

Two are better than one,
    because they have a good reward for their toil.

Behold, what I have seen to be good and fitting
   is to eat and drink
   and find enjoyment in all the toil with which one toils.

Everyone also to whom God has given wealth and possessions
    and power to enjoy them,
and to accept his lot and rejoice in his toil—
   this is the gift of God.
For he will not much remember the days of his life
   because God keeps him occupied with joy in his heart.

Let your garments be always white.
   Let not oil be lacking on your head.
Enjoy life with the wife whom you love. . . .
Whatever your hand finds to do,
   do it with your might.

Light is sweet,
   and it is pleasant for the eyes to see the sun. ▪

following: Jan Brueghel the
Elder, *Village Festival*, 1612

139

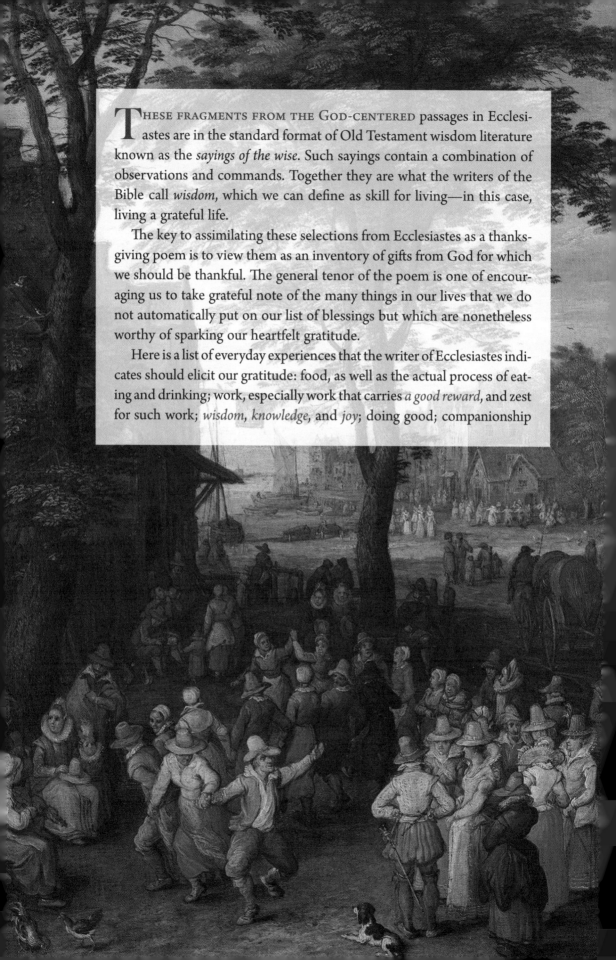

THESE FRAGMENTS FROM THE GOD-CENTERED passages in Ecclesiastes are in the standard format of Old Testament wisdom literature known as the *sayings of the wise*. Such sayings contain a combination of observations and commands. Together they are what the writers of the Bible call *wisdom*, which we can define as skill for living—in this case, living a grateful life.

The key to assimilating these selections from Ecclesiastes as a thanksgiving poem is to view them as an inventory of gifts from God for which we should be thankful. The general tenor of the poem is one of encouraging us to take grateful note of the many things in our lives that we do not automatically put on our list of blessings but which are nonetheless worthy of sparking our heartfelt gratitude.

Here is a list of everyday experiences that the writer of Ecclesiastes indicates should elicit our gratitude: food, as well as the actual process of eating and drinking; work, especially work that carries *a good reward*, and zest for such work; *wisdom*, *knowledge*, and *joy*; doing good; companionship

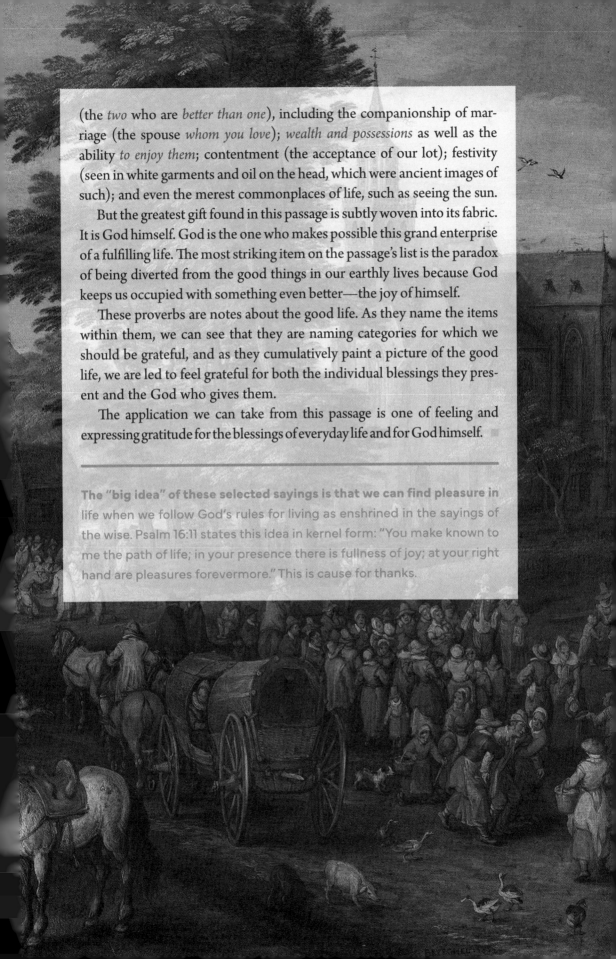

(the *two* who are *better than one*), including the companionship of marriage (the spouse *whom you love*); *wealth and possessions* as well as the ability *to enjoy them*; contentment (the acceptance of our lot); festivity (seen in white garments and oil on the head, which were ancient images of such); and even the merest commonplaces of life, such as seeing the sun.

But the greatest gift found in this passage is subtly woven into its fabric. It is God himself. God is the one who makes possible this grand enterprise of a fulfilling life. The most striking item on the passage's list is the paradox of being diverted from the good things in our earthly lives because God keeps us occupied with something even better—the joy of himself.

These proverbs are notes about the good life. As they name the items within them, we can see that they are naming categories for which we should be grateful, and as they cumulatively paint a picture of the good life, we are led to feel grateful for both the individual blessings they present and the God who gives them.

The application we can take from this passage is one of feeling and expressing gratitude for the blessings of everyday life and for God himself. ◼

The "big idea" of these selected sayings is that we can find pleasure in life when we follow God's rules for living as enshrined in the sayings of the wise. Psalm 16:11 states this idea in kernel form: "You make known to me the path of life; in your presence there is fullness of joy; at your right hand are pleasures forevermore." This is cause for thanks.

Come, Ye Thankful People, Come

HENRY ALFORD (1810–1871)

Come, ye thankful people, come,
Raise the song of harvest home:
All is safely gathered in,
Ere the winter storms begin;
God, our Maker, doth provide
For our wants to be supplied:
Come to God's own temple, come,
Raise the song of harvest home.

All the world is God's own field,
Fruit unto his praise to yield;
Wheat and tares together sown,
Unto joy or sorrow grown:
First the blade, and then the ear,
Then the full corn shall appear:
Lord of harvest, grant that we
Wholesome grain and pure may be.

For the Lord our God shall come,
And shall take his harvest home;
From his field shall in that day
All offences purge away;
Give his angels charge at last
In the fire the tares to cast,
But the fruitful ears to store
In his garner evermore.

Even so, Lord, quickly come
To thy final harvest home;
Gather thou thy people in,
Free from sorrow, free from sin;
There forever purified,
In thy presence to abide:
Come, with all thine angels, come,
Raise the glorious harvest home. ■

EVEN THOUGH THIS HYMNIC POEM ranges widely from the explicit theme of the November Thanksgiving celebration, it is firmly ensconced on the short list of hymns that are sung at traditional Thanksgiving services in the United States and is thus a Thanksgiving hymn by usage and custom. Its opening line is doubtless one reason for this tradition. This line is first of all a conventional call to worship, such as we might find in the Psalms. A summons to *come* (here repeated for emphasis) is a hymnic convention, as the index within a typical hymnbook will quickly confirm. This poem's own summons to come is specifically a summons to assemble for a thanksgiving worship service in a church (which it metaphorically calls a *temple*). Just as the Old Testament's calls to praise typically name the audience to whom they are being issued, the audience here is named as *ye thankful people*, which is appropriate to the occasion.

The remainder of the poem's opening stanza places the implied congregational gathering at a time of annual harvest. Thanksgiving in a rural setting always includes gratitude for harvest. The author of "Come, Ye Thankful People, Come" was British rather than American, and his phrase *harvest home* draws on British country rituals that are much older than the American Thanksgiving. All this suggests that the experience of taking stock of God's provision, and of being thankful for it, is universal. The poem's first stanza speaks of God our Maker supplying *our wants* or needs, which is the essence of thanksgiving.

George Melvin Smith, *There Was a Vision*, no date;
following: John Martin, *Gleaners in the Wheat Field*, 1847

After the conventional thanksgiving features of the opening stanza, the poem takes an unexpected turn. By a process of association, its description of an annual harvest of crops expands into a constellation of harvest passages that are found in the New Testament. The poem merges these references into a metaphoric picture of human life as a *field* that bears a *harvest,* symbolic of living in a world in which people must accept or reject salvation in Christ. Stanza 2 is an appeal to God to help us to bear a *wholesome* harvest of belief, stanza 3 warns that the final harvest is momentous for either good or ill, and stanza 4 offers a prayer for Christ to usher in the heavenly bliss of the redeemed. Even though the import of stanzas 2–4 is far removed from the subject of a physical harvest of crops, agricultural imagery is so palpably present within them that, at a subliminal level, they never totally leave the harvest season behind.

The hymn travels a long distance from its opening call for us to gather for a harvest festival or a Thanksgiving church service at the end of November, but that does not mean that the poem as a whole is not a thanksgiving poem. By the time we assimilate the entire work, the gratitude we are moved to express is not primarily for a physical harvest of crops but rather for our citizenship in God's spiritual kingdom.

Our takeaway from this poem is double: we can accept its winsome opening call to join in corporate thanksgiving at *God's own temple,* and we can be thankful for having the prospect of being part of a spiritual harvest in the life to come. ▪

This hymn brings together the ideas of physical blessing in the world of agriculture and our need to choose to live as citizens of God's spiritual kingdom. Deuteronomy 11:13, 15 does the same: "If you . . . love the LORD your God and . . . serve Him with all your heart and all your soul, . . . He will give grass in your fields for your cattle, and you will eat and be satisfied" (NASB).

A Thanksgiving Poem

PAUL LAURENCE DUNBAR (1872–1906)

The sun hath shed its kindly light,
   Our harvesting is gladly o'er;
Our fields have felt no killing blight;
   Our bins are filled with goodly store.

From pestilence, fire, flood, and sword
   We have been spared by your decree,
And now with humble hearts, O Lord,
   We come to pay our thanks to thee.

We feel that had our merits been
   The measure of your gifts to us,
We erring children, born of sin,
   Might not be now rejoicing thus.

No deed of ours hath brought us grace;
   When you were nigh our sight was dull;
We hid in trembling from your face;
   But you, O God, were merciful.

Your mighty hand o'er all the land
   Has still been open to bestow
Those blessings which our wants demand
   From heaven, whence all blessings flow.

You have, with ever watchful eye,
   Looked down on us with holy care,
And from your storehouse in the sky
   Have scattered plenty everywhere.

Then lift we up our songs of praise
    To you, O Father, good and kind;
To you we consecrate our days;
    Be yours the temple of each mind.

With incense sweet our thanks ascend;
    Before your works our powers pall;
Though we should strive years without end,
    We could not thank you for them all. ∎

IN KEEPING WITH PAUL DUNBAR'S bent toward folk literature, the format of this poem is simple and straightforward. Its diction is traditional and old-fashioned, as is its stanzaic form, which is known as the *quatrain* (a four-line stanza that rhymes *abab*). Its dominant structure is exactly what we expect from a thanksgiving poem: a catalog of blessings that have been received. The first six stanzas contain the catalog of benefits before the word *Then* marks a pivot at the beginning of the seventh stanza. This too is expected—after a rehearsal of blessings, a thanksgiving poem turns naturally to an actual expression of thanks to God.

A closer look reveals a pleasing abundance of complexity within the poem to balance its simplicity. For example, when we tabulate its direct addresses to God (which include the pronouns *you* and *your*), we find no fewer than sixteen, alerting us that the entire poem is conceived as a prayer addressed to God. Although an expression of thanks is largely reserved for its two-stanza conclusion, it is foreshadowed by the second pair of lines in stanza 2. Again, the poem's dominant element is a wholly positive account of everything that has transpired in the life of the nation during the preceding year, yet two whole stanzas (3 and 4) are devoted to a confession of our sin and our unworthiness to receive God's favor. Finally, interwoven throughout the catalog of blessings is a continuous thread of ascribing them all to God—the source *whence all blessings flow*.

The record of the year's events in the speaker's life and that of his nation is idealized in the extreme. According to the poem, nothing bad has happened. To quote a famous pair of lines from a play by Robert Browning, "God's on his throne; all's right with the world." When we encounter such unmitigated optimism about the state of the world, we naturally wonder whether the optimist is naive or out of touch with reality.

An excursion into an author's biography is often a good starting point for dispelling such skepticism. Dunbar was a Black American who faced all the typical discriminations against his race. On the death of Laurence's younger sister at the age of three, his father abandoned the family. For the last six years of his life, before his death at the untimely age of thirty-three, Dunbar was stricken with steadily worsening tuberculosis. So our suspicion that the poet's assertions are facile or glib turns out to be unwarranted. The author knew all about human suffering.

No work of literature says all that can be said about a given area of life. It is instead a distillation of material from a broader reservoir. In this

Jules Pascin, *Group of Figures with Boy Holding Flowers*, ca. 1919

poem, Dunbar distills all that is good in life and thanks God for it. A poem about time in the book of Ecclesiastes (3:1–8) tells us that there is a time for every matter under heaven—a time for the good and a time for the bad. Thanksgiving is a time to celebrate what is good in our lives.

The lesson for us to learn from this poem is that we should be grateful to God for the good things that he has sent into our lives while remaining undeterred by our awareness that life has a contrary side as well. ∎

Psalm 147 is just like Dunbar's poem in that it is an exuberant list of God's blessings that avoids any distracting inroads into negative territory. Verses 12–13 of this psalm read,

> Praise the LORD, O Jerusalem!
> 　　Praise your God, O Zion!
> For he strengthens the bars of your gates;
> 　　He blesses your children within you.

Thomas Eakins, *The Banjo Player*, ca. 1877

Giving Thanks to the Father for You

SELECTIONS FROM COLOSSIANS 1

We always thank God,
    the Father of our Lord Jesus Christ,
when we pray for you,
since we heard of your faith in Christ Jesus
    and of the love that you have for all the saints,
    because of the hope laid up for you in heaven.

Of this you have heard before in the word of the truth,
    the gospel, which has come to you,
as indeed in the whole world it is bearing fruit and
       increasing—
    as it also does among you,
since the day you heard it
    and understood the grace of God in truth.

And so, from the day we heard,
    we have not ceased to pray for you,
asking that you may be filled with the knowledge of his
       will
    in all spiritual wisdom and understanding,
so as to walk in a manner worthy of the Lord, fully
       pleasing to him:
    bearing fruit in every good work
    and increasing in the knowledge of God;

being strengthened with all power,
   according to his glorious might,
     for all endurance and patience with joy;

giving thanks to the Father,
   who has qualified you
     to share in the inheritance of the saints in light.

He has delivered us from the domain of darkness
   and transferred us to the kingdom of his beloved Son,
in whom we have redemption,
   the forgiveness of sins.

And you, who once were alienated
   and hostile in mind,
     doing evil deeds,
he has now reconciled in his body of flesh
   by his death,
in order to present you holy and blameless
   and above reproach before him. ■

A passage from later in Colossians sums up what has been presented above: "Therefore, as you received Christ Jesus the Lord, so walk in him, rooted and built up in him and established in the faith, . . . abounding in thanksgiving" (2:6–7).

A T THIS LATE POINT IN our anthology, we may think that everything that can be said about thanksgiving, and about the formats by which it is expressed, has already been covered, but in fact this epistolary thanksgiving contains much that is new. It is the first entry we have seen in which an author thanks God for the people he knows. These people are Christians. At once a model begins to take shape in our minds: we can and should thank God for fellow Christians. The author tells the recipients of his letter that he gives thanks for them *when [he and Timothy] pray for you.* This is a helpful reminder that all thanksgiving that is expressed to God is an act of prayer.

Most of the entries in this anthology express thanksgiving for the physical and social blessings of everyday life—a thanksgiving that is often placed into an annual cycle during which people take stock of the blessings of each year that is drawing to a close. The thanksgivings within the New Testament epistles stand out by virtue of their single-minded focus on the spiritual life of redemption in Christ. This selection from Colossians does not follow a strict topical structure but is instead fluid in its arrangement. From its intermingling of topics, we can discern those of giving thanks for forgiveness of sin, growing in faith and understanding, being empowered to live a sanctified life, and receiving a place of eternal inheritance in heaven. The governing motif is the riches that believers possess in Christ.

Not everything in the passage is phrased in terms of thanksgiving for fellow believers. A more universal principle is at work. If we stand back far enough so as to take in the entire picture, we can see that every part of it names an aspect of the Christian life that we ourselves have received. Every line—including every line of petition—names a spiritual reality that we possess through Christ, and thus every line awakens our gratitude. The lyric quality of upsurging emotion, which is so characteristic of the New Testament epistles, adds to the feeling of uplift that we feel as we read this passage.

The takeaway is to allow the passage to prompt us to absorb anew what we possess in Christ—including our fellow believers—and then to express our thanks for this to God. ▪

Carlo Saraceni,
Paradise, ca. 1598

Giving Thanks When Our Station in Life Is Modest

Thomas à Kempis (1380–1471)

O Lord, grant me to be mindful of your benefits, both general and special, with great reverence and diligent meditation, that thus I may be able worthily to give you thanks. I know that I cannot render to you due thanks for even the least of your mercies. I am unworthy of all the good things that you have given me, and when I consider your majesty, my spirit fails because of the greatness thereof. All things that we have in soul and body, and whatsoever things we possess, whether outwardly or inwardly, naturally or supernaturally, are your good gifts, and prove that you, from whom we have received them all, are good, gentle, and kind. . . .

All things come from you. Therefore in all things you should be thanked. You know what is best to be given to each person. Why this person has less, and that more, is not for us but for you to understand. . . . Wherefore, O Lord God, I reckon it a great benefit not to have many things that bring praise and glory outwardly and after the thought of men. . . . Nothing should so much rejoice the one who loves you and knows your benefits as your will in him, and the good pleasure of your eternal providence, wherewith he ought to be so contented and comforted that he would willingly . . . be held of small and low account . . . [rather than] to be more honorable and greater in the world than others. For your will and the love of your honor ought to go before all things, and to please and comfort him more than all benefits that are given or may be given to himself. . . .

Be thankful, therefore, for the smallest blessing, and you shall be worthy to receive greater. Let the least be unto you even as the greatest, and let that which is of little account be unto you as a special gift. If the majesty of the Giver be considered, nothing that is given shall seem small and of no worth, for that is not a small thing that is given by the Most High God. . . . Whoever seeks to retain the favor of God needs to be thankful for the favor that is given, and patient in respect of that which is taken away. Let him pray that it may return and be humble so that he lose it not.

God is generous in giving us the grace of comfort, but people do ill in not giving God thanks for it. Thus the gifts of grace are not able to flow unto us, because we are ungrateful to the Author of them, and do not return them wholly to the fountain from whence they flow. For grace always becomes the portion of him who is grateful, and God takes it away from the proud and gives it to the humble.

The saints of God are those who . . . ascribe to God all the good that they have received, . . . and they desire that God shall be praised above all things. . . . Therefore, give thanks to God for his grace. ■

T HIS PASSAGE'S THOUGHTS ON THANKFULNESS come from one of the most famous books in history. Multiple sources claim that *The Imitation of Christ* is the best-selling and most widely translated book after the Bible. Its author, Thomas à Kempis, was a monk of Dutch-German extraction. His book consists of a hundred individual meditations that cover the whole of the spiritual life and include chapters titled "Of Gratitude for the Grace of God" and "Of the Recollection of God's Manifold Benefits."

This entry fills a niche not only in this anthology but also, more generally, in our thinking about gratitude. It should be viewed as asserting a solution to a problem. The problem is how we can be thankful if we are people of modest means. Earlier ages spoke quaintly of "the mean estate," by which they meant the situation of possessing average or even below-average ability, social standing, or income level. Many a culture inclines us to regard success and wealth as a blessing and the lack of them as a curse. Advertising, of course, plays into this materialistic success ethic, but it is also an inherent bent of the human soul to think in such terms. Once we understand that Thomas à Kempis is responding to a specific problem, his remarks fall readily into place as giving us reasons to be thankful for small gifts and modest means. He offers three reasons for us to be grateful even if we own little.

First, we should have a humble estimate of ourselves. We are not entitled to an abundance or excess of good things. We should therefore be grateful for whatever God's grace and favor send us. Second, everything that we attain, including seemingly small achievements, are gifts from a beneficent God. Anything that this *good, gentle, and kind* God gives us deserves to be received with thankfulness. Conversely, nothing that comes from such a God should *seem small and of no worth*.

His third reason forms the most prominent part of this passage: spiritual possessions, and the gift of God's grace, have greater value than external prosperity. In fact, Thomas hints that external prosperity can obscure people's gratitude for spiritual blessings. As an incentive for us to heed his words, Thomas offers the thought that if we are grateful for small blessings, and if we value the spiritual more than the physical, then we will qualify for larger blessings.

What we should take away from this passage is that we need to confront, instead of ignore, our common tendency to think that only success and wealth merit our gratitude, and to resolve to be grateful for all that God sends—especially his gifts of grace. ■

When reduced to its core, this passage asserts that everything we receive is a cause for gratitude because (1) it comes from a good God and (2) nothing can compare with the spiritual blessing of his grace. Psalm 136:1 is of similar import: "Give thanks to the LORD, for he is good, for his steadfast love endures forever."

David Teniers the Younger, *Peasants Dancing and Feasting*, ca. 1660

Giving Thanks for God's Providence

PSALM 23

The Lord is my shepherd; I shall not want.
    He makes me lie down in green pastures.
He leads me beside still waters.
    He restores my soul.
He leads me in paths of righteousness
    for his name's sake.
Even though I walk through the valley of the shadow of death,
    I will fear no evil,
for you are with me;
    your rod and your staff,
    they comfort me.
You prepare a table before me
    in the presence of my enemies;
you anoint my head with oil;
    my cup overflows.
Surely goodness and mercy shall follow me
    all the days of my life,
and I shall dwell in the house of the Lord
    forever. ∎

Surely this is the most famous lyric poem in the world. Even though we may not normally think of it as a thanksgiving poem, we experience it as such. Before we consider why, we need to look closely at the poem itself.

Psalm 23 belongs to the genre known as *pastoral literature*. This means that the psalm's frame of reference is the shepherd's life. Following the widespread literary archetype known as the *green world*, a pastoral poem evokes the rural landscape of sheep, pastures, and water. The activities portrayed in a pastoral poem are those that a shepherd performs during the course of a typical day. Psalm 23 further belongs to a specific pastoral category known as the *ideal day*. Such a poem traces a shepherd's daily routine as he cares for his sheep, and it recreates the events of the day in loving detail.

Of course Psalm 23 is not primarily about shepherds and sheep. It uses them as metaphors for the human condition. We need to be clear about how metaphor works—starting with the fact that the term itself is based on the Greek word that means "to carry over." Metaphor secures its effect by comparing one thing (level A) to something else (level B). But its full meaning emerges only if we experience level A at the fullest possible extent before we carry over its meaning to another level. This means that we need to enter completely into the green world of Psalm 23 and its depiction of a good shepherd caring for his sheep. Overall, the actions it describes trace a daily journey from a sheepfold, over treacherous terrain to a place of grazing and drinking, and then to a midday rest in a peaceful oasis, before returning at the end of the day to the sheepfold.

Thomas Gainsborough, *Pastoral Landscape*, ca. 1783

What a shepherd does for his sheep, God also does for his people. We absorb that meaning as we carry over the references regarding sheep to a human level. For every detail about shepherding in the poem, we should ask and answer the question, What is something God does for us that corresponds to this detail about the life of a shepherd and his sheep? The controlling theme of the poem is providence, and it emphasizes the sufficiency of God's provision. By the time we come to the end of the psalm, we have covered all of life—both physical and spiritual.

But how is this a thanksgiving poem? As we contemplate the ways it shows us the shepherd providing for his sheep, and the corresponding ways in which God provides for us, feelings of gratitude automatically well up within us. And as they do, we can scarcely avoid turning this gratitude into an expression of thanksgiving to God.

The takeaway this psalm offers us is that we can revel in the world's greatest poem, contemplate the sufficiency of God's provision for us, and turn in thanksgiving to the Good Shepherd of our lives. ■

The shepherd in Psalm 23 is a good shepherd. Jesus' Good Shepherd discourse takes the psalm's theme to a still higher level:

> I am the good shepherd. I know my own and my own know me, just as the Father knows me and I know the Father; and I lay down my life for the sheep. (John 10:14–15)

Worthington Whittredge,
Noon in the Orchard, 1900

All People That on Earth Do Dwell

WILLIAM KETHE (DIED 1594)

All people that on earth do dwell,
Sing to the Lord with thankful voice;
Him serve with fear, his praise forth tell;
Come now before him and rejoice.

Know that the Lord is God indeed;
Without our aid he did us make;
We are his flock that he does feed,
And for his sheep he does us take.

O enter then his gates with joy,
Within his courts your thanks proclaim;
Let thankful songs your tongues employ;
O thank and magnify his name.

Because the Lord our God is good;
His mercy is forever sure;
His truth at all times firmly stood,
And shall from age to age endure. ■

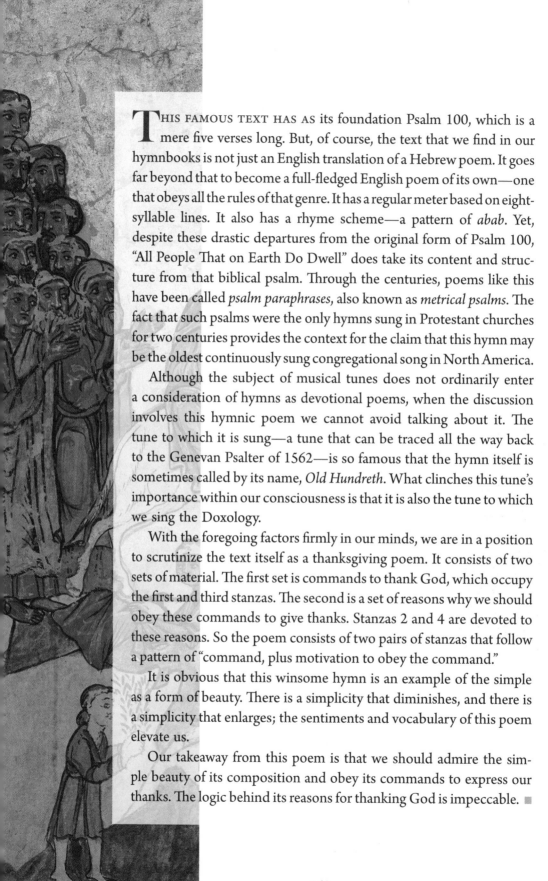

Ｔ	HIS FAMOUS TEXT HAS AS its foundation Psalm 100, which is a mere five verses long. But, of course, the text that we find in our hymnbooks is not just an English translation of a Hebrew poem. It goes far beyond that to become a full-fledged English poem of its own—one that obeys all the rules of that genre. It has a regular meter based on eight-syllable lines. It also has a rhyme scheme—a pattern of *abab*. Yet, despite these drastic departures from the original form of Psalm 100, "All People That on Earth Do Dwell" does take its content and structure from that biblical psalm. Through the centuries, poems like this have been called *psalm paraphrases*, also known as *metrical psalms*. The fact that such psalms were the only hymns sung in Protestant churches for two centuries provides the context for the claim that this hymn may be the oldest continuously sung congregational song in North America.

Although the subject of musical tunes does not ordinarily enter a consideration of hymns as devotional poems, when the discussion involves this hymnic poem we cannot avoid talking about it. The tune to which it is sung—a tune that can be traced all the way back to the Genevan Psalter of 1562—is so famous that the hymn itself is sometimes called by its name, *Old Hundreth*. What clinches this tune's importance within our consciousness is that it is also the tune to which we sing the Doxology.

With the foregoing factors firmly in our minds, we are in a position to scrutinize the text itself as a thanksgiving poem. It consists of two sets of material. The first set is commands to thank God, which occupy the first and third stanzas. The second is a set of reasons why we should obey these commands to give thanks. Stanzas 2 and 4 are devoted to these reasons. So the poem consists of two pairs of stanzas that follow a pattern of "command, plus motivation to obey the command."

It is obvious that this winsome hymn is an example of the simple as a form of beauty. There is a simplicity that diminishes, and there is a simplicity that enlarges; the sentiments and vocabulary of this poem elevate us.

Our takeaway from this poem is that we should admire the simple beauty of its composition and obey its commands to express our thanks. The logic behind its reasons for thanking God is impeccable. ■

The preceding hymn and commentary all rest on Psalm 100, and this excerpt from that psalm encapsulates them: "Enter his gates with thanksgiving, and his courts with praise! Give thanks to him; bless his name!" (v. 4).

T'oros the Deacon, *Entry into Jerusalem*, 1311

Notes

MOST OF THE EXTERNAL FACTS that are attached to the poems in this anthology belong to a common storehouse. This information appears in numerous sources, both print and electronic, making it misleading to attach it to a specific source. Whenever information for a given entry is tied to a specific source, or when I judged that a reader might want further details, I have provided a note.

The selections from the Book of Common Prayer were gleaned from different parts and editions of the book and lightly edited by Leland Ryken.

The five Old Testament snapshots of thankfulness in action are taken from Genesis 8:15–16, 18–20; 28:16, 18, 20–22; 1 Samuel 1:20, 25–28; 2:1; 1 Chronicles 29:10–11, 13; Daniel 2:19–20, 23.

John Donne's reflections on Psalm 6 are taken from his sermon on Psalm 6:8–10 (sermon 53) in *The Works of John Donne*, ed. Henry Alford (London, 1839), 2:478–81. The prayer is excerpted from Meditation 8, "The King Sends His Own Physician," in *Devotions upon Emergent Occasions* (London, 1624), 92–93. Both selections have been lightly edited and modernized.

Joseph Addison's essay on God's mercies with an accompanying poem appeared in the August 9, 1712, edition of *The Spectator*, as reprinted in *The Spectator: A New Edition*, ed. Henry Morley (London, 1891), 3:111–13. The texts of the prose piece and poem have been excerpted from their originally longer versions, as well as lightly edited and modernized.

Jan Brueghel the Elder, *Die Ernte (Sommer)*, 1596

The first diary entry from Oliver Heywood, as well as information about thanksgivings in Puritan England, is taken from Horton Davies, *The Worship of the English Puritans* (Dacre Press, 1948; repr., Morgan, PA: Soli Deo Gloria, 1997), 282. All other entries are taken from *The Rev. Oliver Heywood, B. A., 1630–1702: His Autobiography, Diaries, Anecdote and Event Books*, ed. J. Horsfall Turner (Brighouse, UK, 1881), 85, 225, 236, 247, 248, 271, 278, 293. The text has been lightly edited.

In Communal Thanksgivings in Puritan New England, the passage by William Bradford appears in his history of the Plymouth colony titled *Bradford's History "Of Plimoth Plantation"* (Boston, 1898), 94–95, 96–97. Edward Winslow's classic account of the three-day thanksgiving of the Pilgrims appears in *A Journal of the Pilgrims at Plymouth*—a book commonly known by the short title *Mourt's Relation*, ed. Dwight B. Heath (New York: Corinth Books, 1963), 82, 83–84. William Bradshaw's statement appears in "A Marriage Feast," reprinted in *Two Marriage Sermons* (London, 1620), 14. The quotation from John Calvin is taken from *Calvin: Institutes of the Christian Religion*, ed. John T. McNeill, trans. Ford Lewis Battles, vol. 1, *Books 1.i to III.xix* (repr., Philadelphia: Westminster, 1977), 3.10.2. C. S. Lewis's gloss on Calvin's formula *good cheer* appears

Franz Ludwig Catel, *First Steps,*
ca. 1820–25

in *English Literature in the Sixteenth Century Excluding Drama* (Oxford: Clarendon Press, 1954), 35.

Jane Crewdson's poem "You Whose Bounty Fills My Cup" was first published, under the name "I Will Bless the Lord at All Times," in the author's collection of poems titled *Lays of the Reformation, and Other Lyrics, Scriptural and Miscellaneous* (London, 1860), 283–84. The text as printed in the present anthology has been lightly edited, and the pronouns modernized. The biographical data and quotation presented in the commentary come from Charles S. Nutter and Wilbur F. Tillett, *The Hymns and Hymn Writers of the Church: An Annotated Edition of the Methodist Hymnal* (New York: Eaton and Mains, 1911), 402.

The entry from Jonathan Edwards on natural and gracious gratitude is a condensed version of an expansive argument in *A Treatise Concerning Religious Affections*, first published in 1746 and today widely available in web and print editions. The text has been lightly edited.

The congregational thanksgivings on specific occasions were taken from the 1662 edition of the Book of Common Prayer. The text has been very lightly edited.

John Calvin's comments on the need for public thanksgiving appear in his commentary on Psalm 22:22; see John Calvin, *Commentary on the Book of Psalms*, trans. James Anderson, vol. 1 (Edinburgh, 1845), 378. The oft-quoted aphorism from Aristophanes that "high thoughts must have high language" comes from lines 1058–59 of his play *Frogs*. Milton's magical formula "set the affections in right tune" appears in his description of the effects of Christian poetry in the second book of *The Reason of Church Government Urg'd against Prelaty* (1641).

The Magnificat is taken from Luke 1:46–55 and the Song of Zechariah from Luke 1:68–79.

Sarah Hale's reasons why we need a national Thanksgiving combine excerpts from editorials that she wrote in 1861 and 1864. See Sarah J. Hale, "Thanksgiving Day: The Last Thursday in November," Editors' Table, *Godey's Lady's Book and Magazine*, November 1861, 441, and Sarah J. Hale, "Our National Thanksgiving—A Domestic Festival," Editors' Table, *Godey's Lady's Book and Magazine*, November 1864, 440. The texts have been lightly edited.

The selection from Charles Spurgeon on thankfulness neglected comes from a sermon titled "Where Are the Nine? or, Praise Neglected," printed in *Metropolitan Tabernacle Pulpit*, volume 32 (1886): 707–15. It has been lightly edited.

"Thanksgiving Prayer" is widely ascribed to Ralph Waldo Emerson, but no authoritative evidence for this can be found. As a public domain text, it has been treated with the liberty that public domain hymns are treated, with the title, number of stanzas, and sequencing of stanzas variable from one website to another. The poem as printed in this anthology can be viewed as a representative text. The Puritan quotation is from Richard Bernard, *Ruth's Recompense* (London, 1628), 202–3.

John Calvin's essay on why our prayers must include thanksgiving comes from *Institutes of the Christian Religion*, trans. John Allen, vol. 2 (Philadelphia: Presbyterian Board of Publication, 1909), 3.20.28. The text, including the Scripture quotations, have been lightly edited to enhance their readability.

Daniel C. Colesworthy's "Hymn of Gratitude" is reprinted from *A Group of Children and Other Poems* (Boston, 1865), 83–85.

The passage by Daniel Defoe showing how gratitude transformed a life was taken from *The Life and Adventures of Robinson Crusoe* (London: Seeley, Service, and Company), chapters 6, 8, and 9, available online at https://www.gutenberg.org/files/521/521-h/521-h.htm. The text has been lightly edited.

The origins of the reflections on gratitude are murky, and the aphorisms themselves have evolved over time, a process that has been exacerbated by decades of paraphrase and lax citation. See, for example, the journey of the aphorism attributed to G. K. Chesterton, as described at "Taking Things with Gratitude, and Not Taking Things for Granted," *QuoteInvestigator*, November 28, 2019, https://quoteinvestigator.com/2019/11/28/gratitude/. The common attributions given here should thus be received with a degree of skepticism, although the proverbs themselves may be appreciated for their literary merit.

Kate Wheeler's poem "Thanksgiving" is reprinted from the poet's book *Home Poems* (Nashua, NH, 1897), 95.

The passage from Martin Luther on rendering thanks to our Maker comes from *The Large Catechism*, trans. F. Bente and W. H. T. Dau (St. Louis: Concordia Publishing House, 1921). The text has been lightly edited and modernized.

The following passages comprise the medley from Ecclesiastes on God's gifts: 2:24–25; 2:26; 3:12–13; 4:9; 5:18; 5:19–20; 9:8–10; 11:7.

Paul Laurence Dunbar's "Thanksgiving Poem" was reprinted from *The Complete Poems of Paul Laurence Dunbar* (New York: Dodd, Mead, and Company, 1922), 281–82. The pronouns and verb forms have been modernized.

The selections from Colossians 1 are verses 3–6, 9–14, and 21–22.

The selection from *The Imitation of Christ* by Thomas à Kempis is a composite from Book 2, chapter 10 ["Of Gratitude for the Grace of God"] and Book 3, chapter 22 ["Of the Recollection of God's Manifold Benefits"], from the 1866 translation by William Bentham (London: J. C. Nimmo). The text has been edited and modernized.

Antoine Vollon, *Still Life with Cheese*, ca. 1870s

Image Credits

ALL ARTWORKS IN THIS BOOK have been reproduced in good faith, recognizing copyrights where required. Many images have been cropped to fit the format of this book.

Special thanks are due to the following museums for providing artwork and helpful information: Alte Pinakothek (Munich), Art Institute of Chicago, Barnes Foundation (Philadelphia), Detroit Institute of Arts, Metropolitan Museum of Art (New York), National Gallery of Art (Washington, DC), National Museum of Women in the Arts (Washington, DC), Philadelphia Museum of Art, Smithsonian American Art Museum (Washington, DC), and Walters Art Museum (Baltimore).

 5 James Jacques Joseph Tissot, *Hide and Seek*, ca. 1877, oil on wood, National Gallery of Art, www.nga.gov.

6–8 Camille Pissarro, *The Harvest, Pontoise*, 1881, oil on canvas, Metropolitan Museum of Art, www.metmuseum.org.

 10 Paul Cézanne, *Still Life with a Ginger Jar and Eggplants*, 1893–94, oil on canvas, Metropolitan Museum of Art, www.metmuseum.org.

 13 John Whetten Ehninger, *October*, 1867, oil on canvas, Smithsonian American Art Museum, www.americanart.si.edu.

 14 *The Sargent Family*, 1800, oil on canvas, National Gallery of Art, www.nga.gov.

 17 Jean-François Millet, *The Potato Harvest*, 1855, oil on canvas, Walters Art Museum, www.thewalters.org.

 21 Vincent van Gogh, *Wheat Field with Cypresses*, 1889, oil on canvas, Metropolitan Museum of Art, www.metmuseum.org.

George Henry Durrie, *Winter Scene in New Haven, Connecticut*, ca. 1858

24 *The New Testament, The Book of Common Prayer*, ca. 1636, silk, bullion, silver, and silver-gilt thread on canvas and satin, Metropolitan Museum of Art, www.metmuseum.org.

28 Rembrandt van Rijn, *Jacob's Ladder*, 1655, etching, engraving and dry point, Metropolitan Museum of Art, www.metmuseum.org.

28 Lorenzo Monaco, *Noah*, ca. 1408–10, tempera on wood, gold ground, Metropolitan Museum of Art, www.met museum.org.

29 Peter Paul Rubens, *King David Playing the Harp*, ca. 1627–28, oil on panel, Barnes Foundation, www.collection.barnesfoundation.org.

29 Two-Sided Pendant with Daniel in the Lion's Den, 1200 or later, serpentine, Metropolitan Museum of Art, www.metmuseum.org.

30–31 Edgar Degas, *A Woman Seated beside a Vase of Flowers*, 1865, oil on canvas, Metropolitan Museum of Art, www.metmuseum.org.

32 Marietta Minnigerode Andrews, *Daisies and Queen Ann's Lace*, 1890, watercolor and graphite on wove paper, National Gallery of Art, www.nga.gov.

37 Pierre-Édouard Frère, *Interior with Woman Teaching Child to Pray*, ca. 1819-86, pastel on smooth, moderately thick, gray wove paper, Walters Art Museum, www.thewalters.org.

40–41 Adriaen van Ostade, *The Cottage Dooryard*, 1673, oil on canvas, National Gallery of Art, www.nga.gov.

45 Leopold Bruckner, Fresco in St. Nicholas Church, Trnava, Slovakia, late 1800s, paint on lime plaster, iStock by Getty Images, www.iStockPhoto.com.

46–47 Raphaelle Peale, *Still Life with Cake*, 1818, oil on wood, Metropolitan Museum of Art, www.metmuseum.org.

49 Jennie Augusta Brownscombe, *Thanksgiving at Plymouth*, 1925, oil on canvas, National Museum of Women in the Arts, www.nmwa.org.

50–51 George Inness, *Sunrise*, 1887, oil on canvas, Metropolitan Museum of Art, www.metmuseum.org.

52–53 William Trost Richards, *Indian Summer*, 1875, oil on canvas, Metropolitan Museum of Art, www.metmuseum.org.

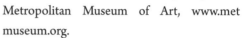

Carducius Plantagenet Ream, *Still Life with Grapes*, no date

56 Jaharis Byzantine Lectionary, ca. 1100, tempera, gold, and ink on parchment, leather binding, Metropolitan Museum of Art, www.metmuseum.org.

57 Medallion with Saint Paul from an Icon Frame, ca. 1100, gold, silver, and enamel worked in cloisonné, Metropolitan Museum of Art, www.metmuseum.org.

58, 60 Isack van Ostade, *The Halt at the Inn*, 1645, oil on panel transferred to canvas, National Gallery of Art, www.nga.gov.

62–63 Willem van de Velde the Younger, *Ships in a Gale*, 1660, oil on panel, National Gallery of Art, www.nga.gov.

64–65 Jan Brueghel the Elder, *River Landscape*, 1607, oil on copper, National Gallery of Art, www.nga.gov.

67 Beaker, 1690/91, silver, Art Institute of Chicago, www.artic.edu.

67 Cup, 9th–10th century, glass, blue-green, Metropolitan Museum of Art, www.metmuseum.org.

67 Cup with geometric decoration, 1st–3rd century, pottery, paint, Metropolitan Museum of Art, www.metmuseum.org.

68 John Frederick Peto, *Breakfast*, ca. 1890s, oil on academy board, National Gallery of Art, www.nga.gov.

70–71 Martin Johnson Heade, *Newburyport Meadows*, ca. 1876–81, oil on canvas, Metropolitan Museum of Art, www.metmuseum.org.

72 Shaikh Zain al–Din, *An Orange-Headed Ground Thrush and a Death's-Head Moth on a Purple Ebony Orchid Branch*, 1778, opaque watercolor and ink on paper, Metropolitan Museum of Art, www.metmuseum.org.

75 Giovanni Larciani (1484–1527), *Sacrifice of Noah (?)*, date uncertain, pen and ink, brush and watercolor, over chalk on cream laid paper, fragments of framing lines in pen and brown ink, Metropolitan Museum of Art, www.metmuseum.org.

76 Anders Zorn, *At Prayer*, 1912, etching, Metropolitan Museum of Art, www.metmuseum.org.

Wolfgang Adam Töpffer, *Young Woman in the Vaudois after the Grape Harvest*, 1821

77 Yokoi Kinkoku, *Catching Fish under Willows in the Rain (Summer)*, ca. 1800, ink and color on silk, Philadelphia Museum of Art, www.philamuseum.org.

78 Jean Honoré Fragonard, *Roman Interior*, ca. 1760, oil on canvas, Metropolitan Museum of Art, www.metmuseum.org.

79 *Girls at Prayer in Church*, 1800s, pencil, charcoal, and chinese white/paper, Walters Art Museum, www.thewalters.org.

81 Célestin François Nanteuil, *Mary and Elizabeth*, 1873, etching, Philadelphia Museum of Art, www.philamuseum.org.

82–83 Francesco Granacci, *Scenes from the Life of Saint John the Baptist*, ca. 1506–7, tempera, oil, and gold on wood, Metropolitan Museum of Art, www.metmuseum.org.

84 Henry Ossawa Tanner, *The Annunciation*, 1898, oil on canvas, Philadelphia Museum of Art, www.philamuseum.org.

87 Eastman Johnson, *Feeding the Turkey*, ca. 1872–80, pastel on wove paper, mounted to canvas on a wooden stretcher, Metropolitan Museum of Art, www.metmuseum.org.

Copy after Isaac van Ostade,
Peasant Family in a Barn, 1640s

88–89 Carducius Plantagenet Ream (1838–1917), *Blackberries Spilling from Tin Cup*, no date, oil on board, National Gallery of Art, www.nga.gov.

90 Winslow Homer, *The Veteran in a New Field*, 1865, oil on canvas, Metropolitan Museum of Art, www.metmuseum.org.

91 Daniel Chester French, *Abraham Lincoln*, modeled 1912, cast after 1912 by Roman Bronze Works, bronze, Art Institute of Chicago, www.artic.edu.

93 Lorenzo Monaco and Matteo di Filippo Torelli, Choral Leaf Fragment: Framed Historiated "S" with Pentecost and Virgin Mary, early 1400s, ink, tempera and gold leaf on parchment, Detroit Institute of Arts, www.dia.org.

95 Master of Morgan 85, *Leaf from Book of Hours: Pentecost with Virgin Mary*, ca. 1515, ink, tempera, and gold on parchment, Detroit Institute of Arts, www.dia.org.

98–99 Johann Baptist Wenzel Bergl, Fresco in Maria Dreieichen Basilica, 1771. Photo: Wikipedia / File: Maria Dreieichen - Fresko a König David .jpg / Wolfgang Sauber / CC BY-SA 3.0 AT. https://creativecommons .org/licenses/by-sa/3.0/at/deed.en. Image has been cropped.

102 Andrea Schiavone, *Christ Standing at the Right Healing the Lepers before Him*, ca. 1545, etching, Metropolitan Museum of Art, www.metmuseum.org.

105 Johann Christian Klengel, *Erntelandschaft* [Harvest Landscape], 1809, oil on canvas, Alte Pinakothek, www.sammlung.pinakothek.de. CC BY-SA 4.0. https://creativecommons.org/licenses/by-sa/4.0/.

106 Model of a Man Plowing, ca. 1981–1885 BC, painted wood, Metropolitan Museum of Art, www.metmuseum.org.

107 Martin Johnson Heade, *Cattleya Orchid and Three Hummingbirds*, 1871, oil on wood, National Gallery of Art, www.nga.gov.

108 The Tree of Life, early to mid 1600s, canvas worked with silk thread, Metropolitan Museum of Art, www.metmuseum.org.

109 Bee-shaped ornament, ca. 918–1392, gold, Metropolitan Museum of Art, www.metmuseum.org.

112 Léon Henri Antoine Loire, *Man, Woman, and Girl at Prayer in Church*, 1864, watercolor and graphite over graphite underdrawing on smooth, moderately thick, beige wove paper, Walters Art Museum, www.thewalters.org.

114–15 David Cox, *Journey Home*, 1833, watercolor with reductive techniques and black chalk, Metropolitan Museum of Art, www.metmuseum.org.

117 *New England Farm in Winter*, 1850 or after, oil on canvas, National Gallery of Art, www.nga.gov.

119 Richard Norris Brooke, *A Pastoral Visit*, 1881, oil on canvas, National Gallery of Art, www.nga.gov.

121 Winslow Homer, *Cannon Rock*, 1895, oil on canvas, Metropolitan Museum of Art, www.metmuseum.org.

122–23 Andreas Achenbach, *Sunset after a Storm on the Coast of Sicily*, 1853, oil on canvas, Metropolitan Museum of Art, www.metmuseum.org.

125 Jean Fouquet, *The Right Hand of God Protecting the Faithful against the Demons*, ca. 1452–1460, tempera and gold leaf on parchment, Metropolitan Museum of Art, www.metmuseum.org.

126–27 Worthington Whittredge, *The Camp Meeting*, 1874, oil on canvas, Metropolitan Museum of Art, www.metmuseum.org.

128–29 Albert Pinkham Ryder (1847–1917), *Harvest*, no date, oil on canvas, Smithsonian American Art Museum, www.americanart.si.edu.

130 Mary Cassatt, *The Map*, 1890, drypoint in brown ink on ivory laid paper, Art Institute of Chicago, www.artic.edu.

131–33 George Inness, *Sundown*, 1884, oil on canvas, Smithsonian American Art Museum, www.americanart.si.edu.

135, 137 Pieter de Hooch, *The Bedroom*, 1658/1660, oil on canvas, National Gallery of Art, www.nga.gov.

140–41 Jan Brueghel the Elder, *Dorffest* [Village Festival], 1612, paint on copper, Alte Pinakothek, www.sammlung.pinakothek.de. CC BY-SA 4.0. https://creativecommons.org/licenses/by-sa/4.0/.

143 George Melvin Smith (ca. 1900s), *There Was a Vision*, no date, tempera, Smithsonian American Art Museum, www.americanart.si.edu.

144 John Martin, *Gleaners in the Wheat Field*, 1847, watercolor with gouache on wove paper, National Gallery of Art, www.nga.gov.

146 Jules Pascin, *Group of Figures with Boy Holding Flowers*, ca. 1919, watercolor, pen and ink, and graphite on wove paper, Barnes Foundation, www.collection.barnesfoundation.org.

148 Thomas Eakins, *The Banjo Player* (study for *Negro Boy Dancing*), ca. 1877, oil on canvas on cardboard, National Gallery of Art, www.nga.gov.

149–50 Carlo Saraceni, *Paradise*, ca. 1598, oil on copper, Metropolitan Museum of Art, www.metmuseum.org.

155 David Teniers the Younger, *Peasants Dancing and Feasting*, ca. 1660, oil on canvas, Metropolitan Museum of Art, www.metmuseum.org.

156–57 Thomas Gainsborough, *Pastoral Landscape*, ca. 1783, oil on canvas, Philadelphia Museum of Art, www.philamuseum.org.

158–59 Worthington Whittredge, *Noon in the Orchard*, 1900, oil on canvas, Smithsonian American Art Museum, www.americanart.si.edu.

160–61 T'oros the Deacon, *Entry into Jerusalem*, 1311, ink and pigments on oriental paper, Metropolitan Museum of Art, www.metmuseum.org.

162 Jan Brueghel the Elder, *Die Ernte (Sommer)* [The Harvest (Summer)], 1596, paint on copper, Alte Pinakothek, www.sammlung.pinakothek.de. CC BY-SA 4.0. https://creativecommons.org/licenses/by-sa/4.0/.

164 Franz Ludwig Catel, *First Steps*, ca. 1820–25, oil on canvas, Metropolitan Museum of Art, www.metmuseum.org.

167 Antoine Vollon, *Still Life with Cheese*, ca. 1870s, oil on canvas, Metropolitan Museum of Art, www.metmuseum.org.

168 George Henry Durrie, *Winter Scene in New Haven, Connecticut*, ca. 1858, oil on canvas, Smithsonian American Art Museum, www.americanart.si.edu.

170 Carducius Plantagenet Ream (1838–1917), *Still Life with Grapes*, no date, oil on canvas, Metropolitan Museum of Art, www.metmuseum.org.

171 Wolfgang Adam Töpffer, *Young Woman in the Vaudois after the Grape Harvest*, 1821, watercolor, over a sketch in graphite or black chalk, Metropolitan Museum of Art, www.metmuseum.org.

172 Copy after Isaac van Ostade, *Peasant Family in a Barn*, 1640s, pen and brown ink, brown and gray wash, and watercolor over traces of black chalk, Metropolitan Museum of Art, www.metmuseum.org.

175 James Peale, *Fruit Still Life with Chinese Export Basket*, 1824, oil on wood, National Gallery of Art, www.nga.gov.

176 Jean Bourdichon, *The Pentecost*, ca. 1480, tempera, granular gold paint, inscribed brown ink, pen and ink, and gilding on parchment, Barnes Foundation, www.collection.barnesfoundation.org.

James Peale, *Fruit Still Life with Chinese Export Basket*, 1824

Scripture Index

Jean Bourdichon, *The Pentecost*, ca. 1480